1951

THE CHARM OF THE CHAPEL

✝

"It is appropriate that the Chapel should be connected by majestic Gothic cloisters with educational buildings on either side"—see page 17.

The
Charm of the Chapel

(Protestant)

By DANIEL L. MARSH

ILLUSTRATED

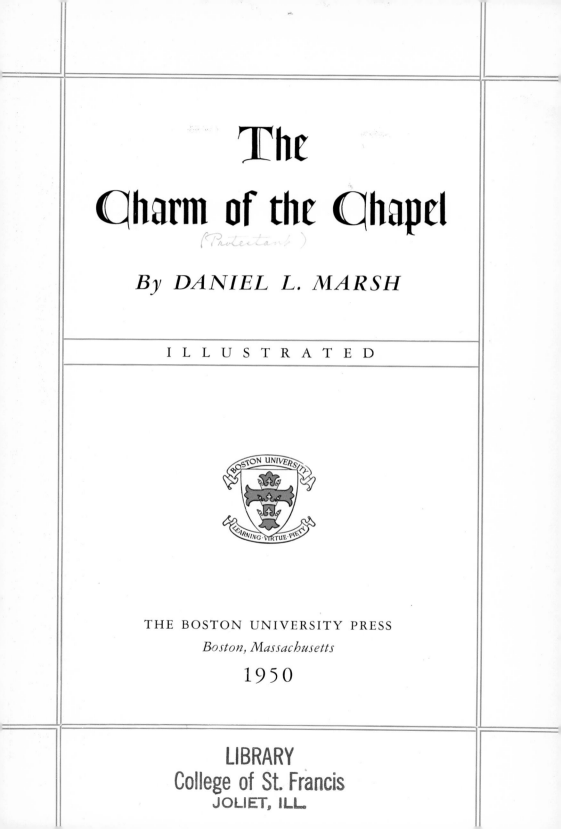

THE BOSTON UNIVERSITY PRESS

Boston, Massachusetts

1950

PRINTED IN U. S. A.

CHARM

*is the quality that attracts irresistibly
and delights exceedingly.*

THIS BOOK

*depicts certain elements of universal
charm in a particular chapel, and is*

DEDICATED
TO MY
CHARMING ARLINE:

*"Blessing is she: God made her so,
And deeds of weekday holiness
Fall from her noiseless as the snow,
Nor hath she ever chanced to know
That aught were easier than to bless."*

CONTENTS

The Universal Element

THE Chapel whose charm this book depicts is a particular building on a particular campus, but its charm is universal. Its appeal to the universal heart of mankind is as valid as the procedures of science in studying the stars or as the heart throb of humanity in a James Whitcomb Riley poem.

Science passes from the particular to the universal. Einstein's theory of relativity states that wherever you are in the Universe, whatever your environment, the same mathematical equations will suffice to describe your observations. The principle of relativity is simply a statement that our local results do indeed have universal validity. Thus theoretical astronomy, for instance, discovers properties of matter, and then reckons that matter in a remote star a billion years ago behaved in basically the same way as matter does today on the earth.

If we pass from science to the humanities, from the material to the spiritual realm, we find that the distinguishing mark of art is its ability to clothe the particular with universality, and the insignificant with significance. The universal element is reason transfigured, reason on fire, reason radiant at every point. This means an enlargement of spiritual boundaries; an escape from narrowness, and prejudice, and littleness.

James Whitcomb Riley is the poet laureate of the American heart because he was able to dig out of the soil of his native Indiana the gold of true poetry. He sang his sweetest songs of the simple, commonplace things that he daily saw and felt. Others might have journeyed to romantic, historic, or classical haunts to find some poetic nugget; but Riley revealed the inner harmony of common things, and made known the musical idea which nature has dressed up in her often rough habiliments. His poetry is an uninterrupted voluntary of the heart. It is the application of ideas to life. The responsive tenderness of his heart has won lettered and unlettered,

[1]

rich and poor, high and low, because it finds its way over the fruitful levels where men are equal. When he was writing, many thought his poems were intensely local, and dismissed them as provincial. Now they know that they are no more provincial than are the poems of honey-lipped Theocritus who sang at the court of Ptolemy Philadelphus sixteen hundred years before Riley sang among the farmsteads of Indiana. He wraps this universality of appeal in an atmosphere of perfect reality. His laughter is whimsical humor that is the common chuckle of humanity. He transmutes private griefs as well as private joys into the great passionate streams of universal suffering within the reach of all men. He confers spirituality and permanence on the fleeting objects of sense. He makes this world the visible symbol of a spiritual power.

I have used Riley's poetry to illustrate what I mean by the universal element in the particular. It is only a short step from *"I,"* *"my,"* and *"me"* to the *"world,"* and the mind flings itself out to the uttermost elements of the human race.

The foregoing explains why people travel from the ends of the earth to look upon Saint Peter's Church in Rome, or to visit the Battlefield of Gettysburg. That explains also why this Chapel, located on a single university campus, has a charm which is bound to make a universal appeal.

Once upon a time a man was nailed to a cross on a skull-shaped hill outside a city wall. It was a local situation, and a commonplace wooden cross; but the Person who died upon it gave it universal significance by flinging wide His arms and lifting all mankind to His Father's heart of love. Ever since then the cross has had in it a universal appeal.

It has been said that "the function of art is (1) to teach us *to see;* (2) to teach us *what* to see; and (3) to teach us *to see more than we see."* This Chapel is art at its highest, — art expressed in architecture, in painting, in sculpture, in stained glass, in line and form, in curve and color. It is my prayer that those who look upon it, and especially those who worship within it, may see all its features of beauty and strength, and that through these several features, they may see more than they see.

[2]

The Architecture — A Vision of Greatness

MORAL education is impossible apart from the habitual vision of greatness." That is one of the most sententious utterances of philosopher Alfred North Whitehead. It is a sentence that leaps at one from the page. To change the word "education" to "progress" would make the utterance equally true and equally arresting: "Moral progress is impossible apart from the habitual vision of greatness."

Every person who is capable and willing to think deeply knows that there is a tragic hiatus between the scientific and technological progress and the moral progress of our age. To say that the world is sick, is only to say what every shrewd and honest observer knows is true; but not everyone can diagnose the nature of its ailment. Medical science tells us that nervous tension is the major cause of peptic ulcers. The present world of tensions appears to have caused peptic ulcers in the body politic — international, national, economic, and political. T. S. Eliot expresses the pessimism of many when he says:

> "Where is the Life we have lost in living?
> Where is the wisdom we have lost in knowledge?
> Where is the knowledge we have lost in information?
> The cycles of Heaven in twenty centuries
> Bring us farther from God and nearer to the Dust."

Education is the indispensable means by which society shapes its ends and determines its progress. There are almost as many definitions of education as there are definers. Every educator in time works out his own definition. Let me give you mine. It is this: *Education is the leading out of the individual into a full-orbed, efficient and rightly integrated personality, — a personality endowed with the spirit of understanding, enabled to express himself fluently and with precision in his mother tongue, equipped to make a living while*

[3]

he lives the more abundant life, serviceable to society, comfortably at home with himself and with his fellows, and en rapport with the ultimate spiritual realities that lie back of the visible phenomena of the universe.

The only way to save society is to save the thinking of the individuals who compose society. Philosopher Whitehead and Poet Eliot both make moral education and moral progress look like panting and gasping anachronisms in the line of march taken by scientific discovery and technological invention.

Recently I came across a reason which had been assigned by a graduate student for his selection of an historical subject for his dissertation. It was this: "As a man suffering from amnesia requires for his cure to be led back into his past, so states need for the understanding of themselves to have their past reconstructed." That is true, to some extent, of states not only but also of organizations, including colleges and universities. Many of the great educational institutions of America are afflicted with amnesia as to the real reasons why they were founded! If they had not been so afflicted, it is conceivable that moral education and moral progress might have kept pace with scientific and technological education and progress.

Our word "moral" is derived from a Latin word which means manner, custom, conduct, or way of life. I am using it to mean both the science and the practice of right conduct, the practical excellence which stems from a person's natural sense of what is right and proper; and to choose and follow the right.

The results of moral lag are found in individuals and organizations, in nations and international conditions. Too often we are not willing to extricate ourselves from the "maddening maze of things" long enough to see realities. Men are drawn hither and yon by visions of satisfied appetite, and lust, and ambition; by visions of achievement, and preferment, and security, yet there is no habitual vision of greatness, and hence no moral progress. There are often fugitive visions of greatness which destroy contentment in those who behold them. True is the old Biblical proverb, "Where there is no vision, the people perish." A less familiar but more accurate translation is: "Where there is no vision, the people run wild."

[4]

"The Architecture is a Vision of Greatness"—see page 6.

There is a delightful English book by Sir George Sitwell entitled *On the Making of Gardens*. In that book Sir George says: "To make a great garden, one must have a great idea or a great opportunity." Not contrariwise, to make a great soul or a great civilization, one must have a great idea and a great opportunity, — and our Chapel furnishes both.

That is the thing we are aiming at in erecting the Chapel at the center of this University campus. We hope that the procession of immortal youth passing through the halls of Boston University for the next thousand years will be vouchsafed a vision of greatness, and that that vision of greatness will become habitual, and result in moral progress. Let me point out some of the elements of greatness which are envisaged by the Chapel.

The architecture itself is a vision of greatness. It is Gothic in style. Gothic architecture was developed from the Romanesque during the hundred years from 1150 to 1250 A.D. It became general throughout Europe, excepting Italy. Fundamentally, it was a matter of engineering. The style evolved from the method of construction. The object was to get a large floor space clear of pillars, and to have churches completely vaulted in stone with ribbed vaults. Thus would they have clerestory windows with large areas for stained glass. Every possible feature that would make the edifice beautiful was added to the simple structural forms.

Goethe, the Shakespeare of Germany, confessed that he was, by hearsay, a sworn enemy of Gothic. And then he speaks of the unlooked-for emotions which surprised him when he beheld the Strassburg Minster: "A sensation of wholeness, greatness filled my soul . . . How often have I come back to enjoy this sacredly profane bliss, to enjoy the gigantic spirit of our elder brethren." The discovery was Wholeness and Greatness — a beauty "by necessity to the smallest part like the trees of God."

If one looks carefully at the architecture of our Chapel, he can see it as a flowering plant deeply rooted in construction and use. There is spiritual significance as well as material. There is a rhythm of marching music in the architectural symmetries of the Chapel. It may be described as the manual prayer of those who designed it

[6]

and built it. There is something timeless and beneficent in it which will continue in spite of all changes in the world at large. It stands for quality and integrity of learning. There is an intrinsic beauty that lends a sort of romantic or transparent glow to the vision. It, flanked by the majestic buildings which house Liberal Arts and Theology, creates an elegant silhouette against the sky. It possesses a compact and unruffled nobility.

Gothic architecture could never have been developed except in an age of faith. It stands for something far above the material needs of any period. It is a composition of stone and glass and steel which makes visible, to those who have eyes to see, the indescribable world of the spirit.

Emerson said that "the Gothic cathedral is a blossoming in stone subdued by the insatiable demand of harmony in man." John Keble says that Gothic architecture is "in comparison with all others, the most beautiful of all, and by far the most in harmony with the mysteries of religion." Schelling regarded Gothic architecture as "music in space, as it were a frozen music," while Madame de Staël says that it "is like a continuous and stationary music."

The way to see our Chapel is to look at it from the south side of Commonwealth Avenue, and then to walk over into the plaza and stand there alone, and let the friendly significance lift your spirit while you contemplate it.

While our Chapel has not the mountain massiveness of the cathedrals of the Middle Ages, yet it holds before the students a vision of greatness. It is a gradation of beauty from foundation up to the tiniest fret, an ensemble of something which creates a rhythm in the vision, something which sings of man's freedom by the truth.

Strength and durability are an essential part of moral progress, and they are also in the vision of greatness vouchsafed by this Chapel. The foundations are driven down forty-five to fifty feet below the surface. The foundation and structural floors are of steel reinforced concrete. The Chapel is built of Indiana limestone. While it was in process of construction, I was talking one day with the engineers and architects, and I inquired, "How long should these buildings stand?" The answer was, "Indefinitely." "But how long?" I insisted.

[7]

Again came the answer: "Indefinitely. Name any time." I replied: "How about five hundred or a thousand years?" And then came the confident answer: "Barring such cataclysms as earthquakes and atomic bombs, these buildings should be in good condition one thousand years from now."

Let the weak-willed person contemplate the vision of strength and solidity, durability and firmness which this Chapel suggests to him, and then let him make that vision habitual, and moral progress for him will no longer be impossible.

Forget not the importance of the *habitual* vision of greatness. The person who has fugitive and sporadic visions of greatness is like the person who stands alone on the deck of the ship at midnight, looking over the deck rail at the waves as they break against the side of the ship where the phosphorescence gleams and sparkles like frightened fireflies caught in the tangle of a trellised vine, — and while the phosphorescence and breaking waves may interest him for awhile, they exert no guiding influence upon him. But the person who has the habitual vision of greatness is like the one who stands on the bridge of the ship, with chart and light and compass, holding conversation with the stars that have broken through the purple shallows of the night, — and there is purpose and meaning in life for him, and the vision lures him on to the destination of moral progress.

Before a stroke of work was done on this campus, we had a master plan for its total development, and that master plan not only included a chapel, but placed it at the center of the campus. We always regarded a Chapel not as a luxury but as a necessity. We have conceived of it as the focal point of the campus. But before a stroke of work was done, we took to heart John Ruskin's words:

[8]

"When we build,
             let us think we build forever,
       Let it not be for present delight
                 nor present use alone:
Let it be such work
          as our descendants will thank us for,
          and let us think
          as we lay on stone,
          that a time will come when those
          stones will be sacred because
          our hands have touched them,
          and that men will say as they look
          upon the labor
          and wrought substance of them,
'See! This our fathers did for us.' "

But there is more to this Chapel than its architecture which gives the vision of greatness. Its stained glass windows — "storied windows richly dight" — fill the Chapel with what Milton called "a dim religious light," and which a French writer says makes you "feel you are in a great reservoir of light and space." The Chapel bestows a still more alluring vision of greatness; for these stained glass windows, "like jewels mounted in delicate and ornate settings of stone," not only cast a burning glow of mysterious and ever-changing light, but they also contain figures that personify the moral greatness of the ages. Who can stand before these windows without being moved by more than the sheer beauty of them? Who can help having the vision of greatness if he will allow himself to meditate upon the character and achievements of such persons as Abraham, Moses, Elijah, and Isaiah; of John the Baptist, Peter, Paul, and Saint John; of Saints Athanasius, Augustine, and Francis of Assisi; of Martin Luther, John Wesley, Francis Asbury, Abraham Lincoln, and Frances E. Willard? Above all, look at the figure of Jesus in the Rose window, or in the great balcony window over the Commonwealth Avenue entrance. Stand before the reredos, and behold the exquisite carvings of Jesus and the four Evangelists, and then think of how they rate to be in this Chapel, and you will find the vision of greatness luring you on to moral progress. And then contemplate

[9]

the Cross on the corner stone, in the Coats of Arms, and surmounting the gable. Study those twelve emblems in the frieze of the Chapel. Let them fire your imagination and wing your faith in the possibilities of moral progress. As you approach the chancel, behold the figures of Jerome, and Wycliffe, and Andrewes upon the lectern, and the heads of Bach and Handel upon the chancel posts. Go down into the Meditation Chapel, and sit in meditative mood before the stained glass windows in which are allegorical pictures of Service, Truth, and Worship. Form the habit of spending much time in the Chapel, and you will have the vision of greatness, and then let that vision become habitual, and moral progress will be possible for you, and, please God, society may experience moral progress because of you.

When King Solomon started to build the temple that had long been in contemplation, he sent word to the King of Tyre, asking for certain materials and help, and in the course of his communication, he said: "The house which I build is great: for great is our God." And a little later in the same communication, he said: "The house which I am about to build shall be wonderful great."

He did not make it great for sake of vanity, display, or ostentation. The reason he made it great was "for great is our God." This is good philosophy. No matter how fine the temple is, the God for whom it is built is greater still. That which is little in man is responded to by what is great in God. Tennyson puts it well:

> "Our little systems have their day;
> They have their day and cease to be:
> They are but broken lights of Thee,
> And Thou, O Lord, art more than they."

"The house which I build is great: for great is our God," said Solomon. That is good theology. "The chief thing about a man is his religion," says Carlyle. Correct! If you have a little conception of God, you will live a mean life. If you have a great God, the vision of greatness will be ever before you. A great God means a great religion, a great worship, a great consecration, a great humanity, and a great vision, which, if it becomes habitual, means moral progress.

[10]

Let the vision of Isaiah become a personal experience for some Boston University students every year: "I saw the Lord, . . . high and lifted up, and his train filled the temple. . . . Then said I, Woe is me! for I am undone; because I am a man of unclean lips, and I dwell in the midst of a people of unclean lips: for mine eyes have seen the King, the Lord of hosts. Then flew one of the seraphims unto me, having a live coal in his hand, which he had taken with the tongs from off the altar: And he laid it upon my mouth, and said, Lo, this hath touched thy lips; and thine iniquity is taken away, and thy sin purged. Also I heard the voice of the Lord, saying, Whom shall I send, and who will go for us? Then said I, Here am I; send me."

At the Center

Inscribed in enduring stone in the Narthex of the Chapel, where they will be seen by every person who enters, are these words:

> LET THIS CHAPEL AT THE CENTER OF THE UNIVERSITY
> CAMPUS SIGNIFY FOREVER THE CENTRALITY BOTH OF
> INTELLECTUAL AND EXPERIMENTAL RELIGION IN EDU-
> CATION AND ALSO OF DEVOTION TO GOD'S RIGHTEOUS
> RULE IN HUMAN LIVES.   — DANIEL L. MARSH

Those words were deliberately phrased, and they tell the whole story not only of the Chapel's location but also of its purpose.

The campus is beautiful for situation. It lies between Commonwealth Avenue and Bay State Road, on the banks of the beautiful and historic Charles River, and extends from Granby Street to University Road, just in town from Boston University Bridge. Its soil is saturated with history. On this site, American soldiers under George Washington, in the Revolutionary War, marched to the shrill call of the fife and the roll of the drum, singing *Yankee Doodle:*

> "Father and I went down to camp
> Along with Cap'n Good'in,
> And there we saw the men and boys
> As thick as hasty puddin'."

"Yankee Doodle" sauntered in the salt marsh meadow which this campus was in the Revolutionary period, for it was immediately adjacent to that important link in the lines of circumvallation in the Siege of Boston, the large and significant "Brookline Fort."

"And there was General Washington upon a strapping stallion, . . . agiving orders to his men" in the self-same three gun-battery

[12]

"The apex of the triangle would be on Boston University's new campus" on the Boston side of the Charles River—see page 14.

which is still extant on the opposite shores of the river. Pelham's "Map of Boston, 1775-1776," shows that the range of the guns of those two forts crossed on our new site. Old Sam Sewall, Chief Justice of the Massachusetts Courts, a later repentant judge in the Salem Witchcraft trials, hero of the old tale of his heavyweight, heavily dressed bride and the pine tree shillings of her father, John Hall, mint-master — he owned at one time the ground which is now Boston University's campus.

It is hard to conceive of any university campus with a more stimulating environment. Within sight, and within walking distance, is Beacon Hill, redolent with stories of the past. Boston has been called "the Athens of America," partly because of the number of statues and monuments which grace its Common, Public Garden, and streets. The most monumented thoroughfare, starting at the Pubic Garden and running right in front of our campus, is triple-width Commonwealth Avenue. Everywhere there are famous literary, historic, and patriotic shrines which verify tradition and vitalize history. This good city is the educational capital of the world. Of its many worthy institutions of higher learning, the three largest are Boston University, Harvard University, and Massachusetts Institute of Technology. If you were to draw an almost equilateral triangle, with the base laid on the Cambridge side of the river, one point resting on the Massachusetts Institute of Technology and the other on Harvard, the apex of the triangle would be on Boston University's new campus.

At the very center of this campus stands the Chapel. The central position was chosen in order that posterity could not misunderstand our conviction concerning the centrality "both of intellectual and experimental religion in education and also of devotion to God's righteous rule in human lives."

Religion is to be intellectually studied, understood, and appreciated. To be acceptable to intelligent young people, religion must be intellectually respectable. Those who teach Religion, or Philosophy of Religion, and kindred subjects should be second to none on the campus in their powers of mental acumen, and, of course, they should "wear through all this tract of years the white flower of a blameless life."

[14]

The intellect is the starting point, but it is not the completion of human nature. Therefore, we call attention to the centrality of experimental religion also in education and in life. Religion is more than mere intellectual assent to creedal dogma: It is a matter of experience and life. True believers can confirm the Bible by their own experience.

The highest knowledge comes to us not along the narrow lane of the intellect but through the broad thoroughfares of the responsive and sympathetic heart. The intellect — clever, boastful, self-idolatrous — may be unsatisfied with its curious questionings and analyses and propositions concerning religion, but the broken and contrite heart may experience the living Saviour's grace and enter the sanctuary of the Divine forgiveness and the Divine complacency.

Therefore, it is our fond hope that our students may be helped by the Chapel to acquire not only the higher education, but also the highest. By way of illustration: Let them study Geography, and let them know by experience the River of Life that flows from the throne of God, and the City whose Builder and Maker is God. Let them study Geology, and let them also take their experimental stand upon the Rock of Ages. Let them study Zoölogy, and let them bow in reverence before the majesty of the Lion of the Tribe of Judah. Let them study Psychology, and let them also become personally acquainted with Him Who knew what was in man, and Whom to know is life eternal. Let them study Botany, and let them also open their souls to the sweet influence of the Rose of Sharon and the Lily of the Valley. Let them study Astronomy, and at the same time let them attain unto the higher knowledge of the Bright and Morning Star and the Sun of Righteousness which has risen with healing in His wings. Let them study the Fine Arts, but at the same time, let them master the art of fine living. Let them study Philosophy, but let them learn also that the highest philosophy is the formula of a perfect life.

Thus will the centrality of intellectual and experimental religion in education lead to God's righteous rule in human life. Reduced to its simplest terms, that means that we are to love God with all our mind, heart, soul and strength, and our neighbor as ourself. We

[15]

must keep step with the Commandments of God against all the forces that oppose us. We must make our attitudes conform to the Beatitudes. We must "seek first the Kingdom of God and His righteousness." We will reverence the sacred value of personality, stand for the essential equality of individual human rights, promote the brotherhood of man as interpreted by the Golden Rule, glorify service as the standard of true greatness, embody faith as the means, and self-sacrificing love as the motive of the Kingdom of God, and will consecrate ourselves to live and work for the domination of ideas, purposes, and intentions of the most lofty and sacred sort.

So we inscribe in stone in the Narthex of the Chapel, for all future generations to see, our profound conviction that vital religion should occupy a central position in any rightly ordered program of education.

All of which is summed up in an epigram by Dupanloup, a French prelate of one hundred years ago, thus: "The soul of education is the education of the soul."

When we leave religion out of our educational program, we practically announce that life can be explained without God, which is the same thing as saying that either God does not exist or is of no consequence. The natural result is to rear a generation of practical atheists who live in an atmospheric pressure of secularism, and whose philosophy of life is crass materialism.

We do not desire that the professors of secular subjects should become propagandists for religion, and certainly much less for any sectarian brand of religion. But we do desire that we shall not be so proud of our knowledge as to forget the need of wisdom. The world's foremost authority on that subject declares that "the fear of the Lord is the beginning of wisdom." The recent history of the world certainly shows that there is need for developing some mechanism of government, of industry, of labor and of management that will gear into the moral imperatives of the Ten Commandments and the Sermon on the Mount.

Timid souls who seek to avoid religious controversy by by-passing the history and literature of the Jewish and Christian religions are worse than foolish and futile: they are emasculators of education,

[16]

which must treat life as a whole. Any education is morally thread-bare which leaves its students unaware of the irreconcilable divergence between good and evil, freedom and necessity, love and self-centeredness, spirit and matter, person and mechanism, progress and stagnation. Expressed in simplest terms, religion means that the individual enters into an offensive and defensive alliance with God, and God is forever on the side of goodness, freedom, love, spirit, person, and progress. The words of Matthew Simpson are still true: "Education without morals is pernicious, and to have morals without religious instruction is impossible." Moral behavior and our democratic institutions are as vitally related to theistic faith as the blossoms and fruit of an apple tree are to its roots.

We believe in and will defend academic freedom even as we believe in and will defend the freedom of religion. But it is my conviction that the two are inextricably interwoven. All advancement in knowledge, all progress in scientific research, all pursuit of truth depend upon academic freedom. But it is the ethical implication of religion that gives to academic freedom a sense of responsibility. Therefore, true religion will never restrict academic freedom, and true academic freedom will never belittle or besmirch the values of religion.

It is therefore most appropriate that the Chapel should be connected by majestic Gothic cloisters with educational buildings on either side — on the east with the College of Liberal Arts, and on the west with the School of Theology. The buildings have been so constructed that a person can start at the Science Laboratories at the easternmost end of the campus, and pass through educational buildings the whole way to the center of the campus, and then through the cloisters into the Chapel, and through the Chapel into the cloisters on the other side, and on through them into the other educational buildings, proceeding to the westernmost end of the development. This is our way of saying architecturally what we strongly feel both academically and morally: that religion will be most effective when it permeates education, and education is most safe when it is infused with the spirit of true religion.

[17]

The Corner Stone

UNDERNEATH the corner stone are two stones from Oxford University, one from St. John's College, and one from Jesus College. The stone from St. John's College was sent to me by the Rotary Club of Oxford, and the stone from Jesus College was sent by the Principal and Fellows of that ancient institution. Why do we have these stones as the very foundation for the chief corner stone of our Chapel? The inscription on the stone from Jesus College answers the question thus:

> "BOSTON UNIVERSITY'S PEDIGREE IS TRACED DIRECTLY
> TO OXFORD UNIVERSITY, ENGLAND
> THIS SUB-CORNER STONE IS FROM JESUS COLLEGE,
> OXFORD UNIVERSITY"

The other stone has this inscription:

[18]

"This stone is from St. John's College, Oxford University"

This line of descent from Oxford will be illustrated and amplified in the descriptions of aisle windows in the Chapel. Suffice it here to say that as Harvard University traces its academic pedigree directly to Cambridge University in England, so also Boston University, more directly than any other fully organized university in America, traces its academic pedigree to the ancient University of Oxford. It is that which gives sentimental value to these sub-corner stones.

On the corner stone is inscribed 1949, the year in which it was laid. Above this date is the Seal of the University. The Seal is a circle, giving on its marginal rim the name of the institution and the year of its founding, 1839, and also the year when it was chartered under its present name, 1869. The entire inner circle is spanned by the Holy Cross, floriated, a symbol of the Christian heritage and aims of the Founders. Central to all is represented in outline the City of Boston, with its culmination in the State House dome. The harbor in the foreground points to the expected service to the whole human world through mutual coöperation in the highest lines of effort.

Inside the corner stone is a bronze box which contains many things which should prove interesting to posterity adown the far-off future. Among these treasures is a copy of the Holy Bible, of the so-called King James translation. One could predict with certainty that no matter when this corner stone is opened, the only novel thing about the Bible will be the date of its printing; for the Book, just because it is what it is, is bound to be in common use millenniums hence. Year after year, the Bible is the world's "best seller," selling in such astronomical numbers as to make the figures for the so-called "best sellers" pale into insignificance.

A knowledge of the Bible is indispensable to anyone who would understand the genius of America, and who would be equipped to defend and perpetuate true Americanism. It is our nation's Sacred Book. The Supreme Court has declared the United States to be a Christian nation. This does not mean that we have, or can have an

[19]

established church, or a tax-supported church; but it does mean that the Bible is the corner stone of our national life.

Practically the only textbook the children of the Puritan settlers of New England had for the first hundred years of their public school system was the Bible. Naturally, they became the moral law-givers of the continent!

The relation of this Book to the very genius of America was accurately expressed by Andrew Jackson, the "Old Hickory" of hero worshipers, who, when dying, placed his hand upon the Bible and said: "That Book, Sir, is the rock on which our Republic rests." The same idea was tersely stated by another soldier-statesmen, U. S. Grant, when he declared: "The Bible is the sheet anchor of our liberties." A hundred quotations from prominent national leaders could be given in support of this thesis, as, for example, the sententious utterance of Daniel Webster: "If we abide by the principles taught in the Bible, our country will go on prospering and to prosper; but, if we and our posterity neglect its instruction and authority, no man can tell how sudden a catastrophe may overwhelm and bury all our glory in profound obscurity."

Our American democracy rests upon the Biblical doctrines of the sacred worth of human personality, the equality of individual rights, brotherhood as interpreted by the Golden Rule, and service as the standard of greatness. All these foundation principles of Democracy are quarried from that bedrock which we call the Bible.

Furthermore, a knowledge of the Bible is indispensable to an adequate comprehension of the great literature of the world. The Bible is itself our supreme literature. The writings of Shakespeare contain 550 Biblical quotations or allusions, and the poetry of Tennyson contains 330 references to the Bible or quotations from it. The speeches of the greatest orators in the English language are interlarded with Scriptural references. The Bible is itself a marvelous library, containing works on history, and biography, and travel, and poetry, and drama, and adventure stories, and love stories, — in fact, no American can claim to be fully educated who is ignorant of the Holy Bible.

Still further, a knowledge of the Bible is indispensable to a proper understanding of the most vital source of the inspiration of great works, noble deeds, and victorious lives. This inspirational value is not limited to the field of literature. It has subdued rude and boisterous minds, and has exercised a creative influence upon those polished arts which have thawed out the ice-locked harbors of human feelings. Music? A whole galaxy of musicians whose names shine on the pages of history like stars blazing in the night found here the inspiration for their greatest works. Architecture? The old cathedrals of Europe are the optimum of architectural splendor, and they are but the materialization of the aspiring moods created by a study of the Bible. Sculpture and painting? The old masters imbibed at the same fountain the motive for their greatest achievements. Archaeology: The sacred volume sends men to study in libraries and archives; to unearth cities long buried; to inspect tombs of ancient kings.

The Bible energizes as well as inspires. One of the historic "Articles of Religion" declares that "the Holy Scriptures contain all things necessary to salvation." This is true concerning both personal salvation and social redemption. Huxley says that the only true education is that which enables a man to do what he knows he ought to do, regardless of the consequences. More than any other book ever written, the Bible communicates power, enabling man to keep step with the commandments of the Almighty against all kinds of opposing forces. No other book so tones up one's personal life as the Bible. It denounces and condemns selfishness and sin, makes resolute the weakened will, wings the faith of the discouraged, comforts the sorrowing, gives hope to the despairing, refines judgment, clarifies reason, purifies imagination, and disturbs the indolent with divine discontent. Worthy of acceptance by everybody is the advice which Abraham Lincoln gave his friend, Judge Speed, namely: "Take all of this Book that you can by reason, and take the rest of it by faith, and you will live and die a better man."

Literally, the Bible is *in* the corner stone of the Chapel. Figuratively, it *is* the corner stone of the Chapel, and of the University, and of any civilization worth saving.

A copy of the Methodist Hymnal, words and music, is in the corner stone, and also a copy of the Book of Discipline, — both donated by the Methodist Publishing House. With these is a copy of the Book of Common Prayer, donated by Bishop Nash of the Protestant Episcopal Church, and a copy of Thomas a Kempis's *The Imitation of Christ,* donated by Archbishop Richard J. Cushing of the Roman Catholic Church, and personally inscribed by him to me. Also in the corner stone is a copy of the Standard Book of Prayer, the Jewish equivalent of the Anglican Book of Common Prayer, donated by the Associated Synagogues of Greater Boston.

These Protestant, Roman Catholic and Jewish books of devotion are meant to symbolize the fact that this Chapel, in its very fundamental conception, is intended to be a house of prayer for all people.

By interesting coincidence, the year in which this corner stone was laid marked the four hundredth anniversary of the first edition of the English Book of Common Prayer, which was ratified by Parliament on the 22nd of January, 1549. The work was accomplished, so stated the Act, "by the ayde of the Holie Ghooste," and "with one uniforme agrement." The Book of Common Prayer has an immense literature. It comprises several of the old service-books. Its revisions began early. The most striking innovation of the Book of Common Prayer was the exclusive use of English. It therefore could be "understanded of the people." This book, Lathbury thought, "was probably more instrumental in furthering the Reformation among the people than even the two Bibles then in circulation." Prayers of this book are applicable today: prayer to be delivered from battle, from pestilence, from privy conspiracy. No less than our forefathers do we need to pray: "We have left undone those things which we ought to have done, and we have done those things which we ought not to have done, and there is no health in us."

Also by interesting coincidence, the corner stone was laid on the Jewish holiday called Sh'vuos — the celebration which commemorates the giving of the Torah to the Children of Israel through Moses on Mount Sinai. Thus members of the Jewish faith were particularly appreciative of the inclusion of their Standard Prayer Book in the corner stone.

[22]

Naturally, many University documents went into the corner stone, such as the General Catalogue, *The Hub* (Student Annual), a little book entitled *Traditions of Boston University,* the Boston University Song Book, and several copies of *Bostonia,* the Alumni Magazine.

Also for the potential posterity of five hundred or a thousand years hence is deposited a copy of a book which I wrote a few years ago under the title of *The American Canon.* Question: Will the seven precious documents which the book contains, and which I expound therein, be vital and precious when this box is opened, or will they be merely "a quaint and curious volume of forgotten lore?"

The corner stone contains also copies of religious journals of all Denominations and secular papers of the week and the day on which the stone was laid.

Many names are preserved for posterity in the hermetically sealed and indestructible bronze box in this corner stone — names in the daily and weekly papers, in the roster of the Boston Rotary Club, in the Hymnal and Discipline and books of devotion, in the *Bostonias,* in the *Boston University News,* in the General Catalogue and *The Hub,* et al!

There is a touch of pathos in the fact that the last poem ever written by William L. Stidger was the one he wrote for the laying of this corner stone. Our generation knows that Professor Stidger was one of the most popular preachers of his time, a prolific writer, a genial and kindly Christian gentleman, and a poet of no mean ability. A copy of his poem, signed in longhand by him, is in the corner stone. It reads as follows:

> With solemn reverence we lay
> This solid corner stone today;
> On slabs from Oxford's ancient walls
> We lift these sacred, holy halls,
>
> With faith in all the years to be
> That man shall find a destiny
> With more of peace, and nobler days,
> In kinder, wider, surer ways;

With hope that from these walls will rise
Majestic beauty to the skies,
A nobler song of ancient good,
A world-wide urge to brotherhood;

Within these walls that there shall shine
A light, Supreme, from the Divine
Through singing windows, clear and bright
A vast, eternal, glorious light.

This chapel through Eternity
Shall rise in splendid majesty,
A symbol of God's love and truth:
That He is dawn, and spring, and youth;

That Education's vast design
Has at its heart the great Divine
Eternal Truth revealed to man
Since time and tides and life began;

That God is at the heart of things;
A dream to which the whole world clings
With frantic hope that there shall be
For man a nobler destiny.

Such is the meaning of these walls,
These altars, cloisters, windows, halls;
Such is the vision that inspires
Our dreams, our hopes, and our desires.

Beside this quiet river here
Shall stand this chapel, tier on tier;
Its Gothic grandeur still to rise
Aspiring toward the stars and skies;

To lift the souls of countless youth
To hope, and faith, and God, and truth;
To fuse the dream within the soul
Into a sound and selfless whole.

Coats of Arms

THE front entrance into the Chapel is by double doors. Above each one of these doors is carved in stone a coat of arms. Over the doorway to the left as you enter, is the Arms of a family, which Arms are described in heraldic terms as: "Gules, a horse's head couped, between three crosses bottonée fitchée, argent." *Gules*

means a red shield; *couped,* cut off smoothly; *bottonée,* a cross that is crossed at three ends or points; *fitchée,* a cross that has the lower end pointed like a dagger; *argent,* that the crosses are white in color (or silver). Translated into ordinary English it would read thus: "A red shield with a horse's head cut off smoothly between three crossed crosses that are white and pointed at the foot." The motto is *"Fidei Coticula Crux,"* which, being translated, is *"The Cross is the touchstone of faith."*

Over the right-hand door as one enters the Chapel is the University's Arms. In heraldic jargon, the description is as follows: *"Argent, a cross fleury Gules,* the three crowns, representing both Oxford University and Boston, England, in pale, and encircling the cross, *Or."* This means: "A

silver or white shield bearing a floriated cross in red (in the case of Boston University, scarlet), the three gold or yellow crowns of old Boston and of Oxford arranged vertically down the shield and encircling the cross."

The Arms of the University are reproduced in color on the artistic chandeliers inside the Chapel. There are eight chandeliers, each one holding six lights. On the circular band to which the lights are affixed, and alternating with the lights, is the Coat of Arms — white shield, on which is the scarlet cross, encircled by three golden crowns. Although so inconspicuous as to be scarcely noticed until one's at-

[25]

tention is called to them, yet the total effect of the forty-eight-fold chaste design and bright color is most pleasing.

The cross is a conspicuous figure on both the University's Arms and the family's Arms. It also, in carved stone, surmounts the Chapel. The Cross is the most wonderful subject that ever appealed to the intellect, the conscience and the imagination of mankind. I do not refer to the Roman gallows; I mean rather the "Cross" which was fashioned in eternity, and whose shadow falls on the disk of the whole scheme of things. I pass from the sign to the thing signified. This Cross condemns a spirit of self-righteousness, even though its wings be crimson-dyed with hues of Paradise. It exalts sacrifice for others. As one life-cell is lost that another may live and grow; as the blossom is sacrificed for the coming fruit; as the mountains are made barren to enrich the valleys; as the soldier gives himself for a principle, a reformer for a cause, and a mother for her child, so the Cross symbolizes in solemn isolation the great truth that we also ought to lay down our lives for others, — as a sacrifice, a devotion, a consecration.

The crowns encircling the cross on the University Arms connect Boston University both with the town of Boston, England, and also with the University of Oxford. The crown has not always been a regal sign. The crown — or coronet, which is a crown of lesser dignity — was originally a wreath of grass or flowers placed upon a general's brow as reward for victory in a battle; or it was a wreath of oak or laurel leaves placed upon the brow of a victorious athlete. In time it came to be a reward for any achievement or distinguished service. The golden ducal crowns on the escutcheon of Boston, England, were not a sign of royalty, but rather a reward for appreciated service. So also the crowns on Boston University's arms have no regal significance: They are merely an heraldic symbol of our inheritance.

The reason why we display a connection on our arms with the first Boston is obvious. We are *Boston* University, taking our name from the City which is our home, albeit we are neither politically controlled nor tax-supported. We are proud of this City, this "Athens of America," the educational capital of this continent, with

[26]

its numerous historic and literary shrines and its many cultural institutions, and with such a distinct lure and charm that merely to live in it is an education to anyone possessed of sufficient intellectual curiosity to pay attention to his environment.

Our fair city of Boston takes its name from Boston, England, because so many of the settlers of our Boston came from the older Boston and its vicinity. The name "Boston" is a contraction of "Botolph's Town." It was derived from a Saxon monk by the name of Saint Botulph. A contemporary spoke of him as "being well-exercised in virtue and holiness . . . He was beloved by all, for he was free from arrogance, being humble, mild and affable in all things. He was a good teacher. In the year 654, he founded a monastery in the water meadow where the River Witham flows into the sea, and as a town developed around his monastery, it was called Saint Botulph's Town, which through long usage became contracted into Saint Botowns and then into Botowns, and finally into Boston.

The crowns also connect us with Oxford University, which dates its beginning from the intellectual awakening which came with the crusades. Since the Oxford University Coat of Arms bears three crowns, it is appropriate that we should have three crowns upon our Arms, indicating our known line of academic descent.

Both the family Arms and the University Arms have the cross, and the latter have golden crowns encircling the cross. The reciprocal relationship of cross and crown was once expressed in an exalted passage by James I. Vance, thus: "The symbol of the Gospel is a cross; but not a cross by itself; not a lone, bare, gaunt, naked cross. The symbol of the Gospel is a crown; but not a crown by itself; not a proud, cold, despotic, selfish, pitiless crown. The symbol of the Gospel is a cross and a crown; a cross lying in a crown; a crown growing around a cross; a cross haloed by a crown; a crown won by a cross."

Over the University's Arms is a ribbon bearing the words, *Boston University*, and underneath is a flowing ribbon bearing the words, *Learning, Virtue, Piety*. These three dynamic words are taken from the Charter. They are the *raison d'etre* of Boston University.

[27]

The Frieze

RUSKIN points out that "ornamentation is the principal part of architecture, considered as a subject of fine art." Anyone who has stood amid the ruins of "the glory that was Greece" has found his gaze transfixed by the fragments of the frieze that adorned the Parthenon. Likewise, in the great Gothic architecture of the Middle Ages, the very genius of which was to set forth emblems and symbols full of meaning, the frieze was always an important part of the ornamentation. Milton, in "Paradise Lost," describes architectural magnificence by saying: "Nor did there want cornice or frieze with bossy sculpture graven."

It is the common practice, in Gothic churches and chapels, to place upon the frieze the emblems of the twelve Apostles. Since we have these emblems in a window of the School of Theology building, which is connected by cloisters to the Chapel, it seemed good to us to design an original frieze for the Chapel. And so we worked out a scheme of ornamentation which is at once beautiful and at the same time indicative of the significance and high-calling of all vocations; for the frieze consists of twelve stones upon which have been artistically engraved emblems of twelve fields of service — professions or occupations — for which the University trains its students.

The proper Christian point of view is that all worthy work is sacred. In some quarters, it is thought that only the man who has been set apart by the imposition of hands for some professional religious work has a holy calling. A backward look across the ages shows certain men who, in hope of attaining holiness, withdrew to caves or monasteries, where they practiced the crucifixion of the flesh, thinking thereby to please God.

Some years ago when I was in Spain, I went out from Barcelona to Montserrat, a bare rock mountain rising abruptly out of the plain (which is but little above sea-level) to an elevation of four thousand

"It seemed good to us to design an original frieze" —see page 28.

feet. On the top of Montserrat is a monastery, — and no other kind of habitation! I asked our guide why the monastery was there. He said it was because the monks were holy men, and they wanted to be near God. I then quoted to him the following poem which I had learned years before, but I am not sure that he caught the real meaning of it:

"The parish priest, of austerity,
        Climbed to a high church steeple
To be nearer God, that he might hand down
        His word upon the people.
So in sermon script he daily wrote
        What he thought was sent from heaven,
And dropped it down on the people's heads
        Two times one day in seven.
In his age, God said: 'Come down and die.'
        And he cried out from his steeple:
'Where art thou, Lord?' And the Lord replied:
        'Down here among my people.' "

Religion inheres in the nature of man, and is vital and intelligent only when it is called forth by the experiences of life.

Take this Chapel as an illustration. When an ordained minister conducts a service within it, nearly everybody would agree that his work is sacred. But what about the janitor who keeps the Chapel clean? And how about the men who toil at the power plant to furnish light and heat for the Chapel? Or look at the construction of the Chapel. Was the work of the men who built this Chapel, if done in the right spirit, any less worthy than the work of the men who will conduct services within it? In the construction of it, the work of the world is represented — architects, and engineers, and clerks, and secretaries; dreamers of dreams, and practical builders, and managers of builders. Common labor excavated and laid foundations, and poured concrete. For it, laborers sweated in steel mills. Other men in Indiana quarried limestone. Others provided the transportation from Indiana to Boston — what a force of men laying and maintaining railroad tracks, building and operating locomotives and freight cars! Artists worked upon stained glass windows and wood carvings and stone crosses, magnificent organ, and sweet-toned carillonic bells. In far-off Italy, in Belgium, in Vermont and Tennessee, men worked in marble quarries, and others transported the result of their toil to Boston. Glass, and paint, and electric wires, and the products of all kinds of human labor have gone into the construction of this Chapel.

I hold that every man's work is sacred if his character is right and his attitude toward his work is holy. The first question is: Is the work worth while? And the second question is: Are the character and attitude of the worker in harmony with the principles of Jesus? The world is God's lumber-yard, His stone-quarry, His forge, His workshop of life, and if we have the right point of view, we are co-workers together with God in building chapels, in raising food to satisfy hunger, in healing the sick, in every kind of work. It is this point of view that gives dignity to trifles. Jesus said: "My Father worketh hitherto, and I work." If we can say the same thing, we link ourselves with the eternal Energy, we coöperate with the lordliest forces in the universe, with fine sequence of heart and joy and value in our work. Our work is the significance of our manhood. It is the expression of our personal life.

Millet's "Angelus," one of the most popular paintings of the last century, shows in the foreground a potato field in which a young man and a young woman, toil-worn peasants, are digging potatoes. On the skyline in the background is the steeple of a church. At the moment which the artist depicts, the Angelus is sounding the call to prayer. The two workers lay aside the implements of their toil, and stand for a moment with bowed heads in silent prayer. That is the proper attitude — where work and prayer are blent like bells of sweet accord. Then comes true the dictum that "to labor is to pray."

And so we have put upon the frieze of this Chapel, emblems under which can be classified practically every kind of worthy work in the world, hoping thereby both to exalt and glorify the world's work, and also to quicken the vision of the workers so that they may behold all work worth doing as holy work if the worker is holy, even as Moses saw the common scrub bush of the desert all aflame with Divine significance.

THE LAMB CARRYING THE FLAG WITH SAINT GEORGE'S CROSS on it has become the emblem of practically all religious work, both professional and lay. The origin of its symbolism is, of course, in the Bible. Many references might be given. Take, for example, Revelation 7:17: "The Lamb which is in the midst of the throne shall feed them, and shall lead them into living fountains of waters."

The figure of the lamb bearing a cross, symbolical of the Saviour as the Lamb of God, found early expression in the liturgies of both the eastern and the western church from the earliest history of Christianity.

The statement that the Lamb is in the midst of the throne indicates that the Lamb rules, but He rules as the Lamb, — the suffering, slain, gentle, merciful, patient Lamb. Also, we are told that the Lamb is the

Shepherd. That means that one who bears the same nature as the flock is the Shepherd of the flock.

Upon the frieze stands this emblem of the whole field of religious work, challenging the service of University students who enter the doors of this Chapel "far down the future's broadening way."

It will always be necessary for some persons to give themselves to the interpretative phase of life, — the work of the ministry, or missions, or some other form of professional religious service. There is scarcely a movement that has meant for the dignifying of manhood and the sweetening of human life that does not stem from such consecration.

But it is not to professional religious work alone that the frieze issues its invitation: It is to all persons who find their chiefest interest in advancing the cause of religion, both as professionals and as lay workers. William James, in his *Varieties of Religious Experience,* declares that "the highest flights of charity, devotion, trust, patience, bravery, to which the wings of human nature have spread themselves have been flown for religious ideals."

There are two irreconcilably divergent philosophies in the world today. The one is crass materialism, which defines the universe as a machine without a Machinist. It regards man as nothing more than a part of the physical universe. What man does, he does in response to physical stimuli. The grave is a blind alley. Death ends all.

On the other hand, you have the spiritual conception of life, which insists that back of the physical phenomena of the universe is a personal God who knows Himself and knows what He is about. Man has a body, but he is a soul. He is responsible for his choices, and can do what he knows he ought to do. The grave is a thoroughfare through which the immortal spirit passes to the bright fields of God beyond.

They are the followers of the Lamb who maintain the spiritual conception of life. At the end, they may rest their tired heads and bruised hearts upon the Good Shepherd.

CALIPERS MEASURING THE EARTH, — here is symbolized the whole field of scientific research and technological invention. The fact that the human mind is able to understand and interpret the laws of nature indicates that those laws are the product of mind, and the name of that Mind is God. A mechanistic view of life and the universe is unreasonable. Matter could not spontaneously have sprung into life, and life could not mechanically have developed into man.

If you should see and hear a musician playing a piece of music, able to understand it, to interpret it, to bring out an intelligent meaning of marks and lines, and dots and dashes written on a piece of paper, you would rightly conclude that the musical score had not "just happened," but that it had been composed by a person. So also the cosmic music is written in a certain way — certain notes follow certain notes. The cause is to be found in the personal Composer, and the name of that Composer is God.

The mind is awe-stricken as the facts of science flash upon it. In whatever direction we look we see unmistakable evidences of wisdom, power, benevolence and design. Since the universe bears the impress of mind, a mind is the only adequate cause of the universe. Only a mind great enough to cause all other existence can be self-existent.

The whole field of scientific investigation and invention merits representation in the Chapel frieze; for keeping up with scientific progress is one way of working with God. The true scientist views the physical universe as a mirror in which he sees God reflected. The pseudo-scientist sees only the burnished surface of the mirror. The person whose spiritual sense is kept alive (and to keep it alive is the function of the University Chapel) is like Agassiz, the scientist, who offered prayer before going upon some new exploration of the universe; like Joseph Henry, one of the greatest physicists of his day, who, after preparing the elements for a new experiment, asked his assistant to remove his hat and to bow his head with Henry, for said Henry, "I have asked God a question and we must wait reverently for the answer;" like Kepler, the astronomer, who said that as he surveyed the wonders of the heavens, he was but thinking God's thoughts after Him; like Linnaeus, the naturalist, who, when he saw a bud unfold into a blossom, said that he had seen God pass before him in glory.

Let the scientist and the technologist enter the Chapel; for it would be tragical to talk learnedly about the mechanism of the universe, but to ignore the Mechanician; to know the garden, but not the Gardener; to enjoy the mammoth painting that we call the cosmos, but to be ignorant of the Divine Artist; to be acquainted with the creation, but not to recognize the Creator.

THE TORCH OF LEARNING illuminating the open book on one side and the laurel wreath on the other is the emblem for the whole field of professional education. The open book represents education in the common acceptation of the term, and the laurel wreath represents physical education.

The teaching profession occupies a central place in social influence It offers an opportunity to interpret the past, to preserve the present, and to determine the future. Every teacher should have an experimental knowledge of religion as well as an intellectual knowledge of the subjects to be taught.

The place of religion in education is so clear to a well-informed person that the merest suggestion should be all that is required. For instance, religion, even in its organized form of the church, has pioneered for education. It has given a sense of responsibility to our much boasted academic freedom. It requires us to make our quest of truth in a spirit of affirmation rather than of negation, of reverence rather than irreverence. It furnishes the necessary synthesis for fragmentary knowledge and fragmentary education. It gives a sense of moral direction, and provides a center and source of moral authority. It establishes a sense of values, showing that which is big as big, and that which is little as little, setting up a hierarchy of ideals under one Lordly ideal. It exalts personality, showing that the individual is the only thing of supreme importance in this world. It glorifies the commonplace, and takes the humdrum drudgery out of the daily grind.

Any wise, forceful, thoughtful, purposeful teacher wields an unlimited power. It is effective, but never spectacular; certain, but hidden; enduring, but not tenuous; obscure, but directive.

What an opportunity to teach mercy, charity, kindness, justice! These are Christian virtues, and the Christian teacher teaches them according to the standards of Jesus. Many children never hear them taught except at school. Many children of this nation never go to Sunday school or to church; but most of them do attend day schools, and here they learn lessons of order, direction, control, and neighborliness that they otherwise would not learn.

Take a special glance at physical education. Both mental and spiritual efficiency are raised or lowered by the physical condition of the body. Therefore, let us have physical education which aims at a sound mind in a sound body. Let education come into the Chapel where it may be guarded and sanctified, including physical education in all its manifestations; for a youth's treatment of his body will be determined by his attitude toward it. Everything will adjust itself if the youth gets clearly before him that the body is the temple of God. It is almost blasphemy against God who dwells within to allow the body to beguile us into lust, anger, selfishness, or unkindness to others.

THE SPINNING WHEEL is used as a symbol of the home and of homemaking. To be sure, a spinning wheel in a modern home is nothing more than an heirloom or an ornament. But it figured in the stern realities of the early days, and has been embalmed in poetry and song.

Is it not appropriate that the multipotent calling of homemaking should be brought into the Chapel and blessed of God? The marriage ritual states that matrimony "is an honorable estate, instituted of God, and signifying unto us the mystical union which exists between Christ and His Church." Every form of religion stresses the sanctity of the home. Roman Catholics call marriage a sacrament. William E. Channing, a leader of liberal Protestantism, spoke of the home as "the nursery of the Infinite," and Charles Parkhurst, a leader of conservative Protestantism, declared that "home is heaven for beginners." Since the hearthstone is the corner stone of society, and since the church, the community, and the state root in the home life, and draw from it to some extent their character, spirit, strength, and safety, it is essential that the home should be religious. The home life should be an oratorio, singing melodies and harmonies of fireside devotion, and of mutual love, service, sacrifice, and sympathy.

Let me share with you the memory of a childhood sense of awareness of God which transfigures and glorifies all life. Our entire family is driving to the little country church. Wild roses along the dusty highway shyly lift their blushing faces as we pass. The meadows are billowy with the crimson foam of clover bloom and are dotted with daisies like the tracks of the stars. The sun has driven his golden chariot up the eastern slopes of space. Pearly clouds with bright oars are rowing across the deep blue sea of heaven. Rocks are hung with tapestries of morning mist. As we turn into the church yard, the horses step with muffled footfall on grassy carpet. At the farther end of the church yard is the little white church, with its spire, like an index finger, pointing our thoughts upward. Back of it is a cemetery where shrubbery and pine keep watch over the everlasting Sabbath of the grave. Now we are within the house of prayer. The sun's rays, filtered through stained glass windows, fill the church with the "dim religious light" of God. Back of the preacher and above him, in the form of an arch, is inscribed the impression Hagar had when, alone and afraid, she wandered in the wilderness: "Thou, God, seest me." As I spell out the words, my soul with reverential awe is filled, and from that day to this, I have felt that my life and work, in public and in private, have been surveyed by the all-seeing eye of God.

My prayer is that students and all other young people might bring their loves and their marriages into the Chapel — or to their respective churches — for the blessing of God, sincerely inviting Him to be the abiding Guest in the homes they establish. Then would they experience this awareness of the Divine Presence, and religion, restored to its rightful place in the home, would once more become relevant and regnant in everyday life.

[39]

THE LYRE, an ancient stringed instrument of music which was considered among Egyptians, Assyrians, and Greeks as the favorite instrument of Apollo, the god of music and poetry, is set up in the frieze as an emblem of music not only, but also of all the fine arts, — architecture, drawing, painting, sculpture, poetry, music, dancing, and the dramatic art. They have engaged mankind's attention for centuries. Every full-orbed program of education includes a bowing acquaintanceship with the fine arts in general, and familiarity with some of them in particular.

This emblem is put on the frieze of the Chapel to indicate to all the world, and to successive generations of students, that if those whose lots are cast in the fields of the fine arts will bring their talents and their lives to God for His blessing, they will find it richly rewarding in many ways. They will discover that the finest of the fine arts is the fine art of living, and that the highest of all the arts is the art of fine living. Then, while pursuing their artistic profession, they will also apply skill and taste to the producing of a fine life according to aesthetic principles. They will design, carve out, execute, a life of marked excellence, worthy of admiration.

Self-expression is the big word with all artists. Self-expression is the expression of one's own personality, as through any creative work. Boasted "self-expression" is sometimes only a euphemism for indecent self-exposure of an unworthy self. Rightly understood, "self-expression" is self-realization, the fulfillment by one's own self of the possibilities of his character or personality. The important thing is to have a self worth expressing.

The self worth expressing has in it something of self-conquest, self-control, self-mastery, self-discipline, and self-sacrifice. Beauty, truth, and goodness are inside before they are outside. Life is real, but reality does not begin and end with the sordid, the sexual, the forbidden. The sewer and garbage are real, but they are not the only reality. There is still a truer truth than any we have yet told. There is a beauty more beautiful than any we have yet produced. There is a goodness surpassing any goodness we have yet practiced. Goodness is Love expressed in conduct; Truth is Love expressed in thought; Beauty is Love in self-expression, in whatever medium.

Self-expression through the art of fine living exerts a finer influence for good than can possibly be exerted by painting, or sculpture, or music, or books. Jesus spoke of a good life, radiantly expressed, as light: "Ye are the light of the world." A candle, by giving itself, sheds light which banishes darkness so that things stand out in their true perspective, and men can see where they are going.

The person who has a self worth expressing is so guided by singleness of purpose that he can say with Saint Paul: "This one thing I do." He might also have Saint Paul's faith: "We know that *all* things work together for good to them that love God." That is real harmony, harmony within one's self, and harmony with the universe. Marcus Aurelius in his *Meditations* says: "All that is harmony for thee, O universe, is in harmony with me as well."

THE LAMP is the emblem of liberal learning, of general culture.
The type used comes from that period of ancient Greece when
objects of utility were also objects of beauty, as we are reminded by
Keats in his *Ode on a Grecian Urn:*

> " 'Beauty is truth, truth beauty,' — that is all
> Ye know on earth, and all ye need to know."

The use of the lamp as the emblem of learning dates from ancient
times, as witness Cowper's *Table Talk:* "Ages elaps'd e'er Homer's
lamp appear'd," or what Cicero said: "Reason, which is, as it were,
the light and lamp of life." It is concerning liberty, the highest
liberal culture, to which Lincoln referred in one of his speeches,
when he said: "I leave you, hoping that the lamp of liberty will
burn in your bosoms, until there shall no longer be a doubt that all
men are created equal."

[42]

By "culture," we mean the development that comes through education, and the enlightenment and refinement of taste acquired by intellectual, aesthetic training. Matthew Arnold declared that the one great passion of culture is "the passion for sweetness and light. It has one even yet greater, the passion for making them prevail."

Some years ago, I wrote to fifteen thousand of the outstandingly successful leaders of American life, asking them to share with me their thoughts concerning character ideals, and then I asked the members of the graduating class of Boston University to do the same thing. Identical ideals, with slight variations in the order in which they were named, were listed by both groups, namely: Honesty, Love, Reverence, Loyalty, Industry, Intelligence, a Moral Sense, Courage, Justice, Self-Control, and Patience. I then asked how they thought these ideals could best be developed in young people. Both groups answered emphatically that example and environment were most important, and that instruction and hero worship stood next. When asked whether they regarded moral and religious training as a necessary basis for the best development of character, two-thirds of both groups answered "Yes, emphatically!"

Let the foregoing explain why cultural learning should be brought into the Chapel for the blessing of God. There is a definite deposit of religious values upon which all reasonable persons of whatever faith should be able to agree. The development of the religious consciousness is essential to sound character. Conduct is character unfolding itself. Emerson reminds us that "Character is higher than intellect. A great soul will be strong to live, as well as to think." Theodore Roosevelt unequivocally declared that "To educate a man in mind and not in morals is to educate a menace to society."

It is impossible to establish society on so solid a foundation that it will automatically remain pure and vigorous. Every generation is faced with the necessity of saving society. It is impossible to capitalize it so strongly that its accumulated moral strength will not subside and ultimately end in bankruptcy unless its strength is renewed in the newer generations. The only sensible thing is to take all our cultural learning into the Chapel for the blessing of God.

[43]

THE VIKING SHIP is the emblem we have chosen for trade and commerce, for the whole field of business and industry. The scepters above it symbolize business and industrial management or administration.

In ancient times, education was only liberal; but the charter of Boston University says that this institution's purpose is, among other things, "the promotion of virtue and piety, and learning in the liberal and useful arts and sciences."

Education in the realm of business and industry is useful, and its usefulness can be determined in terms of money as well as in terms of advancement and various other measurements of success. It evaluates business, and brings business up to the highest excellence of which it is susceptible.

The reason for putting this emblem on the Chapel frieze is to say to all the world that education for commerce and industry, and the management of them, should be brought into the Chapel for the blessing of God. The Prophet Habakkuk tells us of a man who had a successful haul of fish, and then offered incense to his net. There are men like that today. They worship only material success. The bank or store or factory is their temple of worship. The rustle of interest-bearing paper is music to their souls. To them, life consists in the abundance of *things*. Their success is their undoing.

The stress and strife and struggle of our time are industrial and economic for commercial advantage. Our sins are industrial; our injustices are industrial; even vice has been commercialized; political scandals, due to commercial corruption, come and go. Everywhere there is a heart-breaking unrest. Rich men and poor men do not understand each other. Industry absorbs the life of the people.

Woodrow Wilson, the keenest analytical brain that ever occupied the White House, in the last article he ever wrote, pled "like an angel trumpet-tongued against the deep damnation" of selfishness and materialism in the Nation. He urged the removal of the causes of social unrest. He pointed out that these causes lie deeper than "mere economic blunders" or "superficial politics." He concludes in these memorable words:

> "The sum of the whole matter is this, that our civilization cannot survive materially unless it be redeemed spiritually. It can be saved only by becoming permeated with the spirit of our Christ and being made free and happy by the practices which spring out of that spirit. Only thus can discontent be driven out and all the shadows lifted from the road ahead."

Before we can have a Utopia, we must have Utopians. Let the Chapel help to produce educated men and women who represent the attitude and the consequent behavior of Jesus Christ. Thus shall we have leaders of character — "not slothful in business, fervent in spirit, serving the Lord."

THE BALANCES WITH THE SWORD — an emblem which represents even-balanced justice and the determination to defend it — we have put upon the frieze of the Chapel to indicate not only justice in the sense of equity, but also the whole field of jurisprudence and civic service. It is by law that individual conduct is socially controlled. The great Samuel Johnson declared that "The law is the last result of human wisdom acting upon human experience for the benefit of the public."

Justice is a cardinal virtue. It means the maintenance of that which is right. It is the principle of rectitude and just dealing of men with each other. It is the Golden Rule in practice. Sydney Smith opines that "Truth is justice's handmaid, freedom is its child, peace is its companion, safety walks in its steps, victory follows in its train; it is the brightest emanation from the gospel; it is the attribute of God."

[46]

It is right and proper that students who are seeking an education which will enable them to practice law and administer justice, or who are looking forward to a civic or political career, should bring their education into the Chapel for the blessing of God. The larger justice demands this consecration. The rendering of service to civil government is as much a part of the teaching of Jesus as is the rendering unto God the things that are God's. All public servants should recognize themselves as co-workers with God in maintaining order and in advancing and instituting laws in harmony with the Divine idea of progress. Consciousness of this Divine coöperation and responsibility will make impossible malfeasance in office; it will prevent sinister legislation; it will spell the death-knell of corruption in politics.

Ethelbert Callahan, in his little book, *Lawyers and the Bible,* says: "I have gone to the Fountainhead of all law, and lighted my torch in the flame that burned on the brow of Mount Sinai where the Law was given to Moses by the Divine Author of all law." Justinian, Charlemagne, and Alfred the Great each began his more modern code of law by quoting the Ten Commandments. Indeed, the Ten Commandments are, as it were, the "master clock" at the capital of mankind's life by which nations set their laws, and every good man his conduct.

The surest means of national defense and security is expressed in the Bible thus: "The horse is prepared against the day of battle; but victory is of the Lord." When Henry V had won his great victory at the Battle of Agincourt, he asked the chaplain to read a passage from the Bible, and when the chaplain read that noble utterance in the Psalms: "Not unto us, but unto Thy name, O Lord, be the glory," Henry V got down off his horse and all his generals dismounted, and all the great host of his army fell prostrate upon their faces as they shouted together: "Not unto us, not unto us, but unto Thy name, O Lord, be the glory."

THE CADUCEUS AND THE LAMP and the tree of life superimposed upon and growing out of the cross of Christ, we have placed in the frieze as emblems of the whole field of medicine, nursing, and health. The caduceus, sometimes called the staff of Aesculapius, is a familiar symbol. In its earlier form, it was a rod entwined with two serpents, with heads meeting at the top. To this traditional emblem, we have added a lamp in order that the nursing profession might not be forgotten in its ministry of healing. The lamp is used because Florence Nightingale, with a lamp, made her way by night through the miasma of Crimean hospitals.

We have added a third symbol: the tree of life. We deem it appropriate; for in the apocalyptic vision of the "New City," "the tree of life" which grows in the midst of the city, produces leaves that are for the healing of the nations, and its twelve kinds of fruit are ripened every month, as a symbol of unceasing productiveness, of varied fruitfulness, and of complete satisfaction. The cross stands both for the rehabilitating work of the Red Cross organization, and also for the sublime element of self-sacrifice for the sake of others.

No story is more thrilling than the evolution of medical science. It has sometimes groped its way through dismal jungles of ignorance and superstition, and again it has struck a clear road that leads to higher levels of scientific knowledge. Little by little, it has passed into the hands of experts until today those experts constitute the faculties in approved schools of medicine.

Let all who enter the field of medicine, or nursing, or health and healing, secure the best professional education possible. Let them be persons of sound moral character, honest, sincere, dependable. Let them be sympathetic, understanding, spiritually-minded. Let them keep themselves in the best of condition by abstinence from alcoholic beverages and drugs. But most of all, let them regard themselves as co-workers with God.

Jesus Christ is the Good Physician as truly as He is the Good Shepherd. In His earthly ministry, He waged warfare against disease. He made plain the concept of man's life as a unity with two essential ideas: Man is a compound of matter and spirit, clay and divinity, perishable body and immortal spirit. The physician, or surgeon, or nurse, or public health officer who recognizes the centrality of religion in his professional equipment will be a conscious, reverent follower of the Great Physician, and will depend upon Him for assistance in many a crucial hour.

Jesus was love incarnate, and the Cross was the crowning revelation of the love of God. The whole process of redemption is love coming from heaven to earth to create and kindle love, and make it triumph over human hearts and lives. Love is the presiding queen over all the Christian graces. Love is the prime fruit of the spirit.

The best physician, surgeon or nurse is the one whose patients have the greatest confidence in him, and the person in whom such confidence is most naturally placed is the one who incarnates goodness and celestial love.

[49]

O UTREACHING HANDS WITH A FLAMING TORCH between them, we have invented as the emblem of all kinds of social service and social work, enlightened and made more efficient by education. This emblem is on the Chapel frieze to say to all the world that outreaching hands, if well-educated, will render a more beautiful and acceptable service if they have been placed upon the altar of God for His blessing. Indeed, all hands should be brought to God for His blessing — the giving hand, the writing hand, the helping hand, the working hand, the sheltering and protecting hand.

There is nothing more pathetic than the practical failure of many well-intentioned persons in the field of service. Many who start off well lose their inspiration. They grow tired and quit. The truth is that all our fine-spun theories of helpful work, and social justice, and economic righteousness, and political purity will fall to the ground without the goad and the spur and the push of a great spiritual passion. Work in social settlements and hospitals; work in city slums and mission fields; works of reform and amelioration are only half-heartedly done unless they are done as under the shadow of the Almighty.

George Frederick Watts, the great British artist, once painted an allegorical picture which he said he had painted "to suggest great thoughts that will appeal to the imagination and the heart, and kindle all that is best and noblest in humanity." He called the painting "The Spirit of Christianity." Its message gripped me mightily when first I saw it in the Tate Gallery in London. It is a picture of a motherly woman, enveloped by luminous clouds, holding her left hand upon her heart in token of tender pity, and reaching her right hand out in open help and protection to a number of little children of different races and colors that nestle on a cloud at her feet, finding shelter in the ample folds of her ruby robes. She is looking up to heaven with earnest gaze, praying to God with unutterable yearning and pathos for the relief of needy ones. Underneath the clouds is a landscape — a sea smooth as glass, across which lie shafts of light from an unseen moon. The receding shore is marked by calmly flowing rivers on whose banks are dimly seen the spires and roofs of a large city.

Watts dedicated his painting "To all the Churches," hoping thus to help them to forget their petty jealousies and fault-findings and dissensions, and to work together for the realization of the ideal which he had tried to express in his picture.

Happy will the world be when all professed followers of the man of Galilee overcome their bickerings and faultfindings and petty rivalries, and get together on the great business of serving mankind. The world will not long misunderstand such a religion as that.

The secret of all humane progress is in the upreach to God and the outreach to man. Since the devotional, worshiping spirit is the inspiration of the ethical, serving spirit, let us keep alive the spirit of worship. That is the meaning of placing upon the Chapel frieze the outreaching hands, enlightened for unselfish service by the torch of learning.

[51]

A STAR, AN OWL, A UNIVERSITY DOOR — these constitute an emblem which we intend should represent all education outside and in addition to the regular formal university work. That is, it is intended to tell those who are part-time students; those who are studying in the evening or in extension courses; those who are pursuing directed adult education, or who are carrying out a program of self-education, — it is intended to say to all such that their education will be enriched in its meaning if they will bring it into the Chapel. They merit and need the blessing of God as much as anybody else, and life will be ten thousand times more meaningful if with all their getting they get understanding, and if they learn that "the fear of the Lord is the beginning of wisdom."

The owl was the emblem of Minerva, the goddess of wisdom and handicraft or invention. The doors of the University indicate educational opportunity. The star stands for night study not only, but also for aspirations and ideals.

It is the bounden duty of first class institutions of higher learning to open doors of opportunity for the multitude to develop the Godlike possibilities within them. By these opportunities, we are helping persons to see that education can never be spoken of in the past tense; for education is a continuing process throughout life. Our world is being ground smaller and smaller every day. Telephone and radio, television and radar, airplanes and atomic bombs have reduced the earth to a neighborhood, and have made of the planet a tight little playground.

Unless the persons who occupy this little "playground" learn how to play together, they will undoubtedly push one another off the planet. Education is the indispensable means by which the sounder knowledge and the better understanding are to be secured.

Much of what ails the world today is due to the fact that mankind has not been able to distinguish between real progress and progress in things; that is, between moral progress and progress in conveniences. Technological invention has outrun social invention. It is the responsibility of education and religion to bring man's social and moral progress up to his so-called scientific progress.

The supreme privilege of our civilization is not the automobile, or radio, or telephone, but books and mind husbandry for all through reading. Carlyle once said that "All that Mankind has done, thought, gained, or been: it is lying as in magic preservation in the pages of Books." Many of the world's most eminent men acquired an excellent education merely by reading, by self-effort, self-discipline, self-schooling.

Unless one puts his heart blood into his work, that work lacks the mark of excellence. A man can have no heart in his work unless his work is in his heart. The ideal is seen in Luther's motto, *"laborare est orare"* — "to labor is to pray."

CLASPED HANDS OVER THE SEAL of Boston University is the last emblem in the frieze. It is intended to represent the whole field of personal and public relations. Let it say to the procession of immortal youth who will pass through the halls of this University throughout the unborn future that their friendships will be exalted and their loves sanctified by bringing them into the Chapel for the blessing of God. It is to say that our business relations will be toned up, and all our public relations will be dignified and sweetened by the introduction of religion into them. It is intended to say that international trade and commerce, and international political and economic relations also can enjoy a durable peace only so long as they are carried on in the spirit of the religion which is symbolized by the Chapel.

Public opinion is the climate in which reciprocal values, services, and attitudes flourish or die. There is in the world a moral sentiment, a grand public opinion which can be so invoked that the most cunning workers of evil will feel that there is in the air an invisible and awful spirit of righteousness, of pity, of humanity, of moral judgment, with which they have to reckon in the final analysis.

The whole purpose of this frieze, with its twelve emblems, is to say that to our college and university education we must add the elements of love, service, sacrifice, and that which is sublime in the soul of man. Therefore, sweet singer, sing, but not for love of gold, lest your voice become metallic. Physician, work not for money or fame, but to assuage human suffering and to drive back the shadow and power of death. Lawyer, remember that eloquence loves sincere lips. Business man, never forget that the plying of your trade is, as Dickens' *Christmas Carol* proclaims, but a drop in the comprehensive ocean of your real business, which is the good of mankind. Peacemaker, move to the solution of problems of labor and race, not on the basis of power or violence, legislation or arbitration, but of love and sympathy. The teacher, let him train young minds for respectability and usefulness. The social worker, let him penetrate the inferno of our great cities to sweeten bitter lives. The writer, let him consecrate to the glorification of right living, the power of drama, the wealth of language, and the music of poetry. Let the statesman quicken the nation by the ennobling power of the Golden Rule, and make the Beatitudes the magna charta of the nation's life. Let the missionary cross the swelling tide to burning tropic and mountain wilds, to lands of fever and miasma, to carry to the ignorant, liberty, intelligence, and religion. Let the minister of the gospel undermine the citadels of sin and proclaim the glory of loving-kindness, justice and righteousness; for in these things God and men delight.

"All noble work," says Carlyle, "is of a religious nature, work is of a brave nature; which it is the aim of all religion to be. All work of man is as the swimmer's — a waste ocean threatens to devour him; if he front it not bravely, it will keep its word. By incessant wise defiance of it, lusty rebuke and buffet of it, behold how it loyally supports him, bears him as its conqueror along."

Statue of John Wesley

THE statue on the front of the Chapel is of John Wesley. It was sculptured by Arcangelo Cascieri, an alumnus of Boston University. When he was commissioned to make the statue, he acquired and read some twenty-one lives of Wesley. Like any good artist, he was determined to *know* what he was doing. He told me that his admiration for Wesley was unbounded. Wesley really became his hero. Looking at this statue, I cannot help recalling a quatrain which John Quincy Adams wrote as he looked upon his own bust, by Powers:

> "Sculptor! thy hand has moulded into form
> The haggard features of a toilworn face,
> And whosoever looks thereon shall trace
> An age of sorrows and a life of storm."

You may wish to compare this statue with word pictures of Wesley left by some of his contemporaries. Kennicott writes of a sermon preached by Wesley at Oxford, thus: "On Friday morning (24th of August, 1744), having held forth twice in private, at five and at eight, he came to St. Mary's at ten o'clock. There were present the Vice-chancellor, the proctors, most of the heads of houses, a vast number of gownsmen, and a multitude of private people, with many of Wesley's own people, both brethren and sisters. He is neither tall nor fat, for the latter would ill become a Methodist. His black hair, quite smooth, and parted very exactly, added to a peculiar composure in his countenance, showed him to be an uncommon man. His prayer was soft, short, and conformable to the rules of the University. His text was Acts 4:31. He spoke it very slowly, and with an agreeable emphasis. When he came to what he called his plain practical conclusion, he fired his address with zeal and unbounded satire."

[56]

"The greatest Englishman of all the centuries"—see page 59.

William E. Blackstone, the great commentator of English law, heard Wesley preach in the famous pulpit of St. Mary's Church in Oxford. He took notes at the time. In them he speaks of Wesley's personal appearance and dignified bearing as he entered the pulpit, dressed in his clerical robe; his fine face, his hair parted so exactly in the middle and combed smoothly and curling down on his shoulders, his self-command, his sparkling eyes, his pleasing voice.

John Nelson heard Wesley preach in Moorfields on the 17th of June in 1739. He writes: "As soon as he got upon the stand, he stroked back his hair and turned his face to where I stood, and I thought fixed his eyes upon me. His countenance struck such an awful dread upon me, before I heard him speak, that it made my heart beat like the pendulum of a clock; and when he did speak, I thought his whole discourse was aimed at me."

Incidentally, many other persons throughout Wesley's career felt that Wesley's glance and gestures said to each listener, "Thou art the man."

John Wesley was born at Epworth, England, on the 17th of June, 1703. Both his parents were the children and grandchildren of Puritan ministers who had been ejected for nonconformity. One of John Wesley's great grandfathers was Rev. John White, who was foremost among the Puritans whose vision and courage made possible the Massachusetts Bay Colony.

Although Wesley's ancestry was nonconformist and Puritan, yet his father had returned to the Established Church, and was Rector of the Anglican Church at Epworth. To the Rev. Samuel and Susannah Wesley, nineteen children were born. Ten of them died in infancy. That left nine children to be brought up in the rectory. John was the fifteenth child, and his brother, Charles, the world's greatest hymn-writer, the eighteenth. His mother, Susannah Wesley, was one of the great mothers of all history. She maintained a Spartan system in the home, but her wonderful womanhood prevented the rigid discipline from making the home a tyranny. She took care of the early education and religious instruction of her children. She made education an adventure, and religion wholesome, natural, and ineradicable.

[58]

If it were desirable to justify placing a statue of Wesley here, it would be pertinent to recall that Wesley was a university man.* He was a preacher to Oxford University, from which Boston University traces its descent. He was one of the greatest men of all time. Once when I was both studying and lecturing at Oxford University, an Oxford don, in a tea conversation, said: "Measured in terms of his influence for good upon mankind, John Wesley was the greatest Englishman of the eighteenth century." Whereupon, another don, a distinguished historian, said: "Why do you limit him to the eighteenth century? I would say that, measured in terms of his service for good upon the world, John Wesley was the greatest Englishman of all the centuries." That same judgment was pronounced by the late S. Parkes Cadman in his address at the dedication, a few years ago, of Wesley's home as a shrine, to which Cadman added that "Wesley was the greatest Protestant who ever lived." Leslie Stephen long ago spoke of John Wesley as "The greatest captain of men of his century." Buckle described him as "The first of ecclesiastical statesmen."

Lord Macaulay said: "The greatest event of the era was the work of Wesley." Leckey, the historian, says: "Wesley's sermons were of greater historic importance to England than all the victories by land and sea under Pitt." The late Dean Hutton of Winchester, England, who wrote a biography of Wesley, declared: "Wesley's influence is as wide and enduring as Napoleon's and more permanent than Bismarck's. His greatness is incontestable and his influence still unimpaired."

The England to which Wesley preached was wallowing in the mire of immorality that followed the return of the Stuarts. England was ignorant, superstitious, and sinful, an easy prey to a flippant and scornful infidelity. There were laws, but they were cruel and ruthless. Anglican churches were presided over by liquor-drinking, fox-hunting parsons whose appointments were more political than religious. Religion was largely a conventional ritual. Unblushing

*Wesley's other connections with Oxford, as well as additional biographical data of interest will be found on later pages in this book in the exposition of the Oxford tower in one of the aisle windows of the Chapel, and also in the Wesley clerestory window of the Chapel.

baseness prevailed in fashionable and political life. Gambling and extravagance were rife. Drunkenness was a source of misery and degradation.

Wesley's indefatigable industry is a good example for us today. He traveled incessantly, covering in the course of his life more than two hundred fifty thousand miles on horseback and in an old-fashioned buggy. He was a counselor long before counseling was a profession, dealing with cases of conscience, settling family disputes, and giving guidance to thousands of persons. He was constantly preaching, sometimes three and four sermons a day, delivering a total of more than forty-two thousand sermons during his ministry, averaging fifteen a week over a period of fifty years. He carried on an extensive correspondence, and wrote or abridged two hundred books. He maintained his classical studies, and had a familiar working knowledge with Hebrew, Latin, Greek, and German. He tells us that he read history, philosophy, and poetry, for the most part on horseback. Once when he was detained in Wales because the tide was over the sands so that he could not cross them, he tells us: "I sat down in an old cottage and translated Aldrich's logic."

Everybody knows that Wesley captured the imaginations and the hearts of the common people of England. He was instrumental in the reclamation and regeneration of thousands of the underprivileged and dispossessed. But not everybody knows that Wesley also exercised an enormous influence among personalities in the upper registers of society. Wesley was so well-read that any intelligent person loved to have conversation with him. He was probably the most omnivorous reader of his day. Old Samuel Johnson, the erudite compiler of the English dictionary, complained because he could not have as much of Wesley's time as he desired. Wesley is spoken of as the "spiritual father" of Lord Shaftesbury. Wesley influenced John Howard in his work of humanizing the whole prison system, and he likewise influenced William Wilberforce and his fellow enthusiasts — Clarkson, Newton, Macaulay, and Sharp — to overthrow slavery through the sheer vehemence of religious conviction.

[60]

Blackstone, the famous commentator on English law, confessed to being profoundly impressed by Wesley.

And so it went: rich and poor, high and low, educated and un-educated, — they were all stirred by Wesley, albeit many of the baser sort were stirred to crude and cruel opposition.

John Wesley was a man of pronounced benevolence. It is said that when his income was thirty pounds a year, he lived on twenty-eight pounds, and gave two to charity. When his income was sixty pounds a year, he still lived on twenty-eight, and gave away thirty-two. When his income had increased to ninety pounds a year, he still lived on twenty-eight, and gave away sixty-two. His slogan was: Make all you can, save all you can, give all you can. One tragic winter when the poor of London were suffering worse than usual, John Wesley, at that time past eighty years of age, trudged through the snowy, slushy streets of London for full five days, and collected (in addition to a cold and fever) two hundred pounds to help the poor. When someone praised him for it, his reply was: "All too little, but something."

The profits on his cheap books enabled him to give away as much as fourteen hundred pounds a year. When he died, he left his chaise and horses, and his clothes, and as has been quaintly said, "a good library of books, a well-worn clergyman's gown, a much abused reputation, and — the Methodist Church!" The Methodist Church is today the largest Protestant Church in the world, and, measured in terms of its adherents as well as its communicant members, it has the largest following of any church of any kind in America.

Wesley was instinctively a scholar; by zeal and conviction, he was an evangelist. His supreme gift was his genius for organization. With it all, he was a reformer who believed both in the reformation of the individual, and also in the reformation of the social order. Green, a highly discriminating historian, speaking of the evangelical revival inaugurated and directed by Wesley, writes in his *History of the English People:* "One of the noblest results of the revival was the steady attempt, which has never ceased from that day to this, to remedy the guilt, the ignorance, the physical suffering, the social degradation, of the profligate and the poor. It was not until the Wesleyan impulse had done its work that the philanthropic impulse began." Was Green justified in making this remark? Let us look for awhile at that great movement started by Wesley. We talk of the blessings of a cheap press. For its beginnings we must go back to Wesley, whose Dictionaries, Histories, Grammars, and Tracts were written for the million — and not for pay. The social value of his tracts may be seen in such titles as "A Word to a Sabbath-Breaker," "A Word to a Drunkard," "A Word to a Smuggler." He was the founder of the "Strangers Friend Society," and his Orphan Houses were the germinant idea that has grown into much of our modern philanthropy. We point with pride to our public libraries, but "Library Loans" were established by Wesley. He opened a free dispensary at the Foundry. He interested himself in law reform, describing a chancery bill as a "foul monster."

The greatest moral, social, and economic movement of our day is the temperance reform — and John Wesley was its advocate before the days of total abstinence societies. And as early as 1797 we find the members of the Methodist Episcopal Conference of Virginia voting not only to abstain from all use of intoxicating liquors themselves but to try to get others to abstain. Wesley threw himself with all his mighty energy into the cause of the slave. The last letter he ever wrote was to William Wilberforce, encouraging him in his fight against slavery, "that execrable villainy which is the scandal of religion, of England, and of human nature." And he condemned American slavery as "the vilest that ever saw the sun." The Methodist revival started by him served as England's chief bulwark against French infidelity and revolutionary zeal. There probably is no institution of our day more freighted with social possibilities than the Sunday-school. Though its founding is commonly attributed to Robert Raikes, in 1783, yet, as Tyerman remarks, a young Methodist lady by the name of Hannah Ball had a Methodist Sunday-school at High Wycomb fourteen years before Robert Raikes opened his at Gloucester; and the first suggestion of the idea that came to Raikes was from another Methodist, Sophia Cook. In 1784 Wesley wrote: "I find these schools springing up everywhere I go. Perhaps God may have a deeper end therein than men are aware of. Who knows but some of these schools may become nurseries for Christians?"

Naturally, he was much engaged in controversy; but he always maintained moderation in dispute. His unfriendly critics agreed that "he kept his temper and his ground." Although Wesley's work resulted in the founding and organization of the Methodist Church, yet he himself remained a member of the Established Church of England until his death, albeit he was bitterly denounced by the conservatives of that communion. But Wesley was charitable in his judgments of others. One of his harshest critics was Bishop Lavington, and yet Wesley received the Sacrament from the hostile Bishop's hands. Father O'Leary of the Roman Catholic Church was once his antagonist, and yet we see Wesley and Father O'Leary sitting down together to a cozy breakfast. Wesley's catholicity was, indeed, extraordinary.

One of the most interesting episodes in ecclesiastical history is the fact — true beyond question — that once when Wesley was preaching in Northallerton, a member of his congregation was a Roman Catholic priest by the name of Watson Adams, whose parish was in Osmotherley. At the close of Wesley's sermon, the priest met him and invited him to come to his community and preach in his chapel — a chapel that had once been the property of the Franciscan friars. Wesley accepted the invitation. He mounted his tired horse and rode with the priest to Osmotherley. It was ten o'clock at night when they reached there, and the villagers had already retired. But the priest and his friends went through the village, pounding on the doors and inviting the people to come to the chapel. They came, and Wesley preached to them. He went to bed at midnight, having traveled that day sixty miles on horseback, and having preached four times; but feeling, as he confides in his journal, "no weariness at all."

The next morning at five o'clock, Wesley preached again in the little Roman Catholic chapel, as he had promised to do when dismissing the congregation the evening before. The chapel was already filled to capacity, and Wesley preached on justification by faith — the doctrinal core of the Protestant Reformation.

Wesley did not love doctrinal controversy. On one occasion, he said: "God has made divinity practical; the devil controversial." His oft-quoted dictum was: "Think and let think!"

The foundation fact of John Wesley's robust piety was his faith in God. He read the Bible as the Divine Word. Prayer was a reality to him. He believed in an overruling Providence. He was wont to say that he read the newspapers to see how God was governing the world.

John Wesley's father, although Anglican, was a sincere and courageous clergyman. When John, at the beginning of his ministry, was denied the pulpits of the Established Church, he stood on the tombstone over his father's grave in Epworth, England, to preach to the neighbors who swarmed about him to hear his message. He preached everywhere. He preached to coal miners at break of day, as they came from the night shift in the pits, and he could observe the effect of his sermons upon them by the way tears plowed furrows through the coal dust on their faces.

Wesley went to Kingswood and preached to a motley crew of grimy-faced, cynical and jeering fellows from the coal mines. Over against their mob violence, Wesley stood and preached. He used strange words for that day: He talked about "forgiveness," "redemption," and "hope." He pictured the love of God for erring men. Soon besooted faces were streaked with white, where tears of remorse flowed. The result was the same as it was everywhere that Wesley went with his evangel, and this was the result, as reported by him somewhat later: "Kingswood does not now, as a year ago, resound with cursing and blasphemy. It is no more filled with drunkenness and uncleanness, and the idle diversions that naturally lead thereto. It is no longer filled with fights and bitterness. Peace and love are there."

So, while Wesley was a university man, and a Preacher to the University, he never lost touch with common life. He knew that the best way to promote virtue and piety was not by some mighty and phenomenal contingency, but by loyalty in the midst of ordinary tasks and duties, realizing always that "the uncommon life is the child of the common day lived in an uncommon way."

Wesley was busy to the last. On the 23rd of February, 1791, when he was nearly eighty-eight years of age, he preached. The next day he wrote a letter to Wilberforce, urging him to carry on his crusade against the iniquitous slave trade. On the 2nd of March, 1791, he died in his home next door to City Road Chapel. His last utterance showed the most sovereign conviction of his life to be strong in death; for with his dying breath he exclaimed: "The best of all is, God is with us."

Four Historic Doorways

THERE is more of poetry than prose in a doorway. It has mystery in it, and distance, and all the elements of tragedy and comedy that enter into poetic conception.

The doorway that is entered by a bride and groom in the rapturous tumult of love, the doorway through which a casket is borne out, — these private joys and private griefs are transmuted into the great passionate streams of universal suffering within the reach of all human beings. The doorway of a train, or of an airplane, or of an ocean-going steamship suggests distance that makes it appeal to the inarticulate poetry of all mankind.

But the doorway of a church! Here is where poetry and history blend like shine and shower in a rainbow. All church doors open upon the past and upon the future; for every church has a past, and the church that has no future is dead behind locked doors. Through the doors of churches, joy, wonder, worship, surge to expression. Through the doors of churches, we perceive a harmony which is beauty, and which is bodied forth in material form. Through the doors of churches passes a pageantry of color, and form, and sound, and stir; of sin and forgiveness; or irrepressible anticipation and yearning found in no other doorways in all the world.

We have chosen four historic doorways to be pictured in the aisle windows on the east side of our Chapel. They represent the ideas and ideals, the aspirations and hopes of multitudes. They are the four most sacred religious shrines known to the children of men.

They are used in the windows of this Chapel as a means of saying to all the world that it is our will and purpose that this Chapel is to be a house of prayer for all people. Here in God's house there shall be no prejudice, nor bigotry, nor narrow sectarianism.

I like to think metaphorically of Christianity as a tree. Growing out of the soil of Judaism, its life-giving root is Jesus. That is scriptural; for Isaiah, in anticipation of the Messiah, said: "There shall come forth a rod out of the stem of Jesse, and a Branch shall grow out of his roots," and Jesus Himself declared: "I am the root and the offspring of David." Poet Pope sings:

"From Jesse's root behold a branch arise,
Whose sacred flower with fragrance fills the skies."

The upright trunk of the tree, nearest the root, is the Apostolic Church. A horticulturist knows that a tree grows both perpendicularly and horizontally. If it is a healthy tree, its foliage-spread above ground must be equal to its root-spread under ground. Sometimes a tree divides or forks naturally, and sometimes because of decay or injury. There is no question but that the Church, from about the sixth to the sixteenth centuries, experienced conditions which affected it much as ice storms and insect injuries sometimes affect trees. It was then that the Church threw out two main branches: One we call the Roman Catholic Church, and the other the Protestant Church. There are also some smaller branches, such as the Greek Orthodox Church; but the two main forks are the Roman Catholic and the Protestant. Upon the Protestant section a number of branches grew, such as the Lutheran Church, on which came other branches, such as Presbyterianism and Congregationalism; then the Established Church of England, and upon it a number of branches, the most prolific of which is the Methodist, — and so the division and subdivision went on. But it is all one glorious tree, growing perpendicularly and growing horizontally. It ill becomes any one branch to speak derogatorily of the others. When anyone makes the boast that the branch to which he belongs is the best, or the only true one, the sufficient answer is to invoke the words of Jesus: "By their fruits, ye shall know them."

Study these aisle windows from right to left; that is, begin at the balcony and move toward the chancel. And as we view them, let us divest ourselves of all intolerance, and view them objectively and historically; for as Quaker William Penn says: "The humble, meek, merciful, just, pious and devout souls are everywhere of one religion and when death has taken off the mask, they will know one another, though the diverse liveries they wore here make them strangers."

[67]

Doorway of King Solomon's Temple

DURING the major part of his reign, King Solomon was a great builder and statesman. His outstanding achievement was the erection of the Temple, built upon an historic hill in the holy city of Jerusalem. Although surrounded by courts where the worshiping congregations assembled, the Temple itself was not large: length, ninety feet; width, thirty feet; height, forty-five feet. You will get a better mental picture of its size if you compare it with Marsh Chapel whose overall outside length is one hundred twenty feet; width, sixty-one feet, and height to the top of the cross, seventy feet, — to the top of the gable, sixty-four feet.

Solomon's Temple was built of marble-like limestone, quarried from nearby Judean hills. A sample is the block underneath the corner stone of Boston University's "Dewey D. and Harry K. Stone Science Building."

Although the Temple was small, yet it was immense in its spiritual signification. Solomon declared: "The house which I build is great; for great is our God." The religious is always greater than the material. The Temple, as the House of Jehovah, was the chief joy of Israel and the glory of the Jewish Economy. It consolidated twelve nomadic tribes into a nation which gave the world its finest moral code and its monotheistic faith.

The doorway, according to the most authoritative scholarship, was like the one pictured in the window. Through it passed ministering priests into this shrine of the Almighty for four hundred years. In front of it and around it surged and sang and wept and prayed multitudinous worshipers for four hundred years. And then it was destroyed by Nebuchadnezzar! But it is to this day an invisible shrine to which devout Jewish hearts turn throughout the whole wide world.

Doorway to King Solomon's Temple.
Star of David is underneath the Doorway.

The Doorway of Saint Peter's in Rome

T HIS is the doorway of the most sacred shrine of Roman Catholics. Indeed, it is a shrine for all Catholics; for the word *catholic* is derived from a Greek term that means universal, and members of the universal Church of Christ of whatever name or sign reverently visit Saint Peter's in Rome.

It is built where early Christians were martyred, and where, according to tradition, the Apostle Peter was buried. It is the Cathedral Church of the Bishop of Rome, popularly called the Pope.

The early history of Christianity was marked by simplicity and lack of display. In time, a system of church government was evolved by which certain persons were called "overseers" or bishops. There were many bishops, but eventually six bishoprics became more important than the others, namely: Jerusalem, Antioch, Ephesus, Alexandria, Constantinople, and Rome. They were equal in power; but the political pre-eminence of Rome as the capital of the civilized world led to the practice of submitting disputes to the Bishop of Rome for arbitration. Naturally from the City's prestige, the bishop resident there derived prestige. By the beginning of the fourth century, Constantine the Great erected a basilica on the spot where Saint Peter's stands today. Its physical deterioration started while the popes were resident in Avignon (1309-1376), which ruin finally reached such a point that, in 1506, a new cathedral — the present one — was started. The greatest of its architects was Michelangelo.

It is the largest church in Christendom, and is one of the most magnificent structures in the world. It might be likened to a city with marble streets and golden sky. It contains forty-four altars, and a whole forest of columns, and three hundred ninety statues. The floor of the cathedral covers five acres. The works of art in painting and mosaics are worthy of their immortal fame.

[70]

Doorway to Saint Peter's Cathedral.
The Arms of the Vatican are in the
lower part of the window.

The Doorway of the Wittenberg Cathedral

THIS schloss kirche is a shrine of Protestantism. It dates from 1439, and stands today much as it was in the time of Martin Luther (1483-1546). It was made famous by Luther's nailing to its door his ninety-five theses.

Luther was well-educated, and a profound Bible student. In 1513, while meditating on Romans 1:16-17, he attained a new appreciation of the doctrine that the just shall live by faith, and experienced a peace of conscience and assurance of acceptance in the sight of God which he had never known before.

His life marks the end of a period of almost unparalleled infamy in the history of the Papacy. It was an era of moral decline, the fruits of which might well bring the blush of shame to all interested in the good name of the Church.

The practice of "indulgence" had grown out of the penitential system of the ancient Church which punished grave sins by temporary exclusion from the sacraments and service of the Church. It mitigated this discipline by permitting the delinquent to make satisfaction in the form of money contributions. This was the so-called "indulgence." In time the practice had become a regular financial expedient for increasing the Papal revenue.* John Tetzel, a promoter for this system, had a favorite saying: "As soon as the coin rattles in the chest, the soul ascends from purgatory to heaven."

Luther attacked the practice on both doctrinal and practical grounds. That is, Luther was a Protestant in the true meaning of the word; for it is derived from the Latin word *protestare,* which means "to bear witness, or to be a witness." Luther both protested against evils in the Church, and was also a witness for such doctrines as justification by faith, the priesthood of all believers, and such other Biblical truths as are held by those who follow in his train.

---

*See *A Popular History of the Catholic Church,* by a distinguished Roman Catholic historian, Philip Hughes, pp. 126-156 ff. Macmillan Company.

[72]

Doorway to the Wittenberg Cathedral,
with the Arms of Wittenberg underneath.

The Doorway of City Road Chapel

C ITY Road Chapel, London, is a shrine of world-wide Methodism, and is a significant historic building for members of any faith.

John Wesley's first church (1739) was "the Foundry," a dilapidated building that Wesley bought and reconditioned to be used as headquarters of the then new Methodist Movement. Out of this "vast uncouth heap of ruin," Wesley made a chapel which would accommodate fifteen hundred persons, together with numerous utility buildings. By 1776-78, "the Foundry" was worn out, and so Wesley built this new Chapel (City Road Chapel), one hundred fifty yards from the old one. Thus City Road Chapel is the Mother Church of world-wide Methodism. The heavier timbers used in its construction were from a British battleship, donated to John Wesley for this purpose by King George III. Every day, on an average, since it was opened, two new Methodist preaching places have been opened somewhere in the world.

Through this doorway passed John Wesley and his dynamic associates in the Evangelical Revival not only, but also an innumerable host of others for the past one hundred seventy years. John Wesley lies buried just behind the Chapel. When a High Churchman asked who consecrated the ground in which he was buried, a truer Christian replied that the bones of the holy man buried there have consecrated it forever.

John Wesley traveled all over England, Scotland and Wales on horseback, and crossed to Ireland scores of times, denouncing sin in high places and in low, and pleading for the conversion of sinners and for the life of perfect love.

Wesley was lied about and traduced and vilified. He was pelted with missiles by mobs composed of ignorant and wicked people. But he went on his way, bearing and forbearing, giving and forgiving, winning converts, and building the Kingdom of God on earth.

[74]

The Doorway to City Road Chapel,
with the Arms of London in the lower
panel of the window.

Four Historic Towers

A TOWER always attracts attention and often fires the imagination. Associations cling to towers like ivy to a wall. Memories of history are awakened by sight of a tower, — as for instance, a citadel battered by Roman legions, or the Tower of London as an engine of torture, or some tower constructed to house a sweet-toned bell, or a cathedral tower built as a material expression of the aspiring soul of man.

A tower in ruins is a sad sight. You feel the pathos in the lines of Pope:

> "Where round some mould'ring tow'r pale ivy creeps,
> And low-brow'd rocks hang nodding o'er the deeps."

But we much prefer to think of the durability and strength of a tower. Dante exhorts:

> "Be as a tower, that, firmly set,
> Shakes not its top for any blast that blows."

Or again:

> "Be steadfast as a tower that doth not bend
> Its stately summit to the tempest's shock."

To design a tower gives an architect his supreme opportunity for the expression of his sense of beauty. What man-made thing could be more beautiful than the Campanile of San Marco in Venice, or the Bok Tower in Florida, or the "Old Stump" in Boston, England? The "Old Stump," as it is familiarly called, is the Tower of St. Botolph's Church. St. Botolph's Church dates from the time of the Norman Conquest, prior to 1090. The present edifice contains stones from the original Norman structure. The tower forms a landmark for forty miles *"per mare et per terram."* To my eye, it is the most beautiful specimen of perpendicular Gothic architecture in the whole wide world.

[76]

There are four towers which are as full of history for Boston University folk as the Taj Mahal is full of beauty for a Mohammedan. Pictures of them in stained glass adorn the aisle windows on the west side of our Chapel. Reading from right to left — that is, from chancel to balcony — they mark the four steps in this institution's academic pedigree. Our purpose in picturing them here is to preserve for posterity a noteworthy tradition. The word "tradition" roots in a Latin word which means *to transmit.* Francis Bacon in the *Advancement of Learning* explained that by tradition or delivery of truth, he meant "expressing or transferring our knowledge to others." As James Moffatt opines, "Tradition links one generation to another, but the link has a lift in it."

It was William Fairfield Warren, the spiritual founder and first President of the University under its present chartered name, who pointed out that no other fully organized American university has a pedigree leading back so directly and vitally to the ancient University of Oxford as has Boston University. Simply stated, the line runs thus: John Wesley was an Oxford man. He appointed Thomas Coke, another distinguished Oxford man, to come to America, and, in coöperation with Francis Asbury, whom Wesley had previously sent here, to organize the Methodist Church. At the same historic Conference where the Church was organized, Cokesbury College was established. One of the graduates of Cokesbury College was Abel Bliss, who became a Senator from Massachusetts. Senator Bliss was a prominent founder of Wesleyan University. The first person ever to register at Wesleyan University was Osmon C. Baker, who became the first professor in the theological institution which was the nucleus of Boston University.

Therefore, the four towers pictured in the aisle windows are of Oxford University, Cokesbury College, Wesleyan University, and Boston University. If the question be asked why the honor claimed here for Boston University should not be given to Cokesbury or Wesleyan, the answer is that Cokesbury no longer exists, and that neither Cokesbury nor Wesleyan ever became a "fully organized university."

[77]

Christch Church College, Oxford

JOHN WESLEY was six years Scholar of Christ Church College, 1720-26; nineteen years Fellow, Lincoln College, 1726 and following: Teacher in Philosophy, Lecturer on Greek Language and Literature, Moderator of Debates, Preacher to the University.

Toward the end of his student days at Oxford, a profound change came over him. During his last year in Christ Church College, he definitely decided to dedicate his life to God.

The "Holy Club" members, of which John Wesley was the leader, were so punctilious in rendering Christian service and so methodical in their religious exercises that they were called "Methodists" by a cynical wit of Christ Church College.

After Oxford: a brief period at the work of a regular clergyman, and another period at missionary work in Georgia — with a sense of futility in it all — and then the epochal meeting in Aldersgate Mission, where his heart was "strangely warmed;" then his evangelistic, reforming, and organizing ministry which resulted in the Methodist Church.

Wesley sent missionaries to America, the greatest of them being Francis Asbury. At the end of the American Revolution, Wesley ordained and sent to America Thomas Coke, graduate of Jesus College, Oxford, A.B., A.M., D.C.L., — a truly great man.

Coke met with Asbury and other Methodist preachers of America in the famous Christmas Conference of 1784, held in Baltimore. There they organized the Methodist Episcopal Church, the first national church organization effected in the new American Republic. The Conference elected Coke and Asbury Bishops; resolved that it was God's design that they should "reform the continent, and spread scriptural holiness over these lands," and then voted to establish a college which they named, in honor of the two Bishops, "Cokesbury College."

[78]

Tower of Christ Church College, Oxford University.
The Arms of Oxford are in the lower panel.

Cokesbury College

O N New Year's Day, 1785, the Organizing Conference of the Methodist Church, meeting in Lovely Lane Chapel, Baltimore, voted to establish Cokesbury College. It was the realization of a dream which had been cherished for a long time by Asbury. Immediately the Bishops and their colleagues began to canvass for funds. Six months later the corner stone and foundation were laid by Bishop Asbury, in fulfillment of the Methodist conviction that "knowledge and vital piety," always go hand in hand. In his sermon Bishop Asbury referred to "streams which should spring from this opening fountain of sanctified learning."

The building, when completed, was constructed of brick. It was one hundred eight feet long, and forty feet wide. It was located in Abingdon, Maryland, "on the summit and center of six acres of land, with an equal descent and proportion of ground on each side."

School work started in December, 1787. It was especially designed for the sons of Methodist ministers, sons of missionaries, orphans, and children of persons who made sufficiently large financial contribution to the College.

The first faculty consisted of three teachers: The Rev. Mr. Heath (who had been recommended by John Wesley), a clergyman in the Anglican Church; Patrick McCloskey, a "well-educated Irishman," and Truman Marsh, a Quaker.

The College building burned down in 1795. It was rebuilt in Baltimore, but burned shortly thereafter.

During its decade of service, Cokesbury College educated a number of boys who became useful and distinguished citizens, including one of the most learned men of his day; three United States senators; a Federal District Judge; a man who "distinguished himself in the United States Navy," and Abel Bliss, Senator from Massachusetts, an important founder of Wesleyan University.

[80]

The Tower of Cokesbury College,
with the Arms of Methodist Bishops
in the lower panel.

Wesleyan University

URING the three decades following the second burning of Cokesbury College, the Methodists directed their creative zeal for education toward the establishment of secondary schools. The most important of these was Wesleyan Academy in Wilbraham, Massachusetts (1824). A leader in the establishment of Wilbraham was Senator Abel Bliss, a graduate of Cokesbury College. He was the second of the incorporators, and the first secretary of its Board of Trustees. In 1831, friends of Wesleyan Academy procured a charter incorporating Wesleyan University at Middletown, Connecticut. The Honorable Abel Bliss, graduate of Cokesbury College, was one of the incorporators and original trustees of Wesleyan. Wesleyan University — which, in spite of its name, was never more than a liberal arts college — is thus the oldest Methodist college in America, founded as such, and with a continuous existence to the present time.

If one is naming the truly great college presidents of America, he must include the names of Rev. Willbur Fisk, Wesleyan's informing genius and first President, and the Rev. Stephen Olin, its second President. They were both Methodist preachers, gifted, versatile, socially efficient, scholarly, educational statesmen.

As at Cokesbury College, so also at Wesleyan, life was somewhat rigorous. Compulsory chapel was held from 5:30 to 6 o'clock every morning. This meant rather early rising in midwinter! The students carried in their own firewood, and made their own fires. Evening prayers were conducted at 5 o'clock by the President. Students were expected to spend the whole evening in their rooms studying. They were not permitted to study anything on Sunday except such subjects as "Evidences of Christianity."

From those early beginnings, Wesleyan has achieved a creditable career, and has rendered distinguished service to church and country.

[82]

Tower of Wesleyan University, with its Seal
in the lower panel of the window.

Boston University

O N the 24th of April, 1839, a number of officers, graduates, and friends of Wesleyan Academy, and of Wesleyan University met in an educational convention in Boston, "to consider the expediency of establishing a Methodist theological institution." The school was opened at Newbury, Vermont, and Osmon C. Baker, the first man ever to matriculate at Wesleyan University, was made the head of the Newbury Biblical Institute, and the first theological professor.

After a short period at Newbury, the school was transferred to Concord, New Hampshire. After twenty years of increasing serviceableness in Concord, it was transferred (in 1867) to Boston, and newly chartered as the Boston Theological Seminary.

Two years later, Isaac Rich, Lee Claflin, and Jacob Sleeper (at the time, President, Vice President, and Treasurer, respectively, of the Boston Theological Seminary; also, all of them Trustees of Wesleyan Academy, and of Wesleyan University) procured a charter incorporating Boston University. They made the Theological Seminary, which had already had thirty years' existence, the first Department of the University under its newly chartered name.

How meaningful these four towers — Oxford, Cokesbury, Wesleyan, and Boston University! Boston University's tower is both history of the past and also history by anticipation. It is a replica of the "Old Boston Stump," the tower of St. Botolph's Church of Boston, England. Before a single one of Boston University's new buildings was designed, this tower was chosen as the architectural motif for the development of our new campus. A model of the "Old Stump" has been placed over the principal doorway of every new building, and a replica of it is to be erected at the center of the campus, and adjoining the north end of the Chapel.

This tower links Boston University to Boston, England.

[84]

The "Old Boston Stump," with the
Arms of Boston University underneath.

The Clerestory Windows

THE clerestory windows — the large upper windows between the balcony and the chancel — were made by America's foremost artists in stained glass, the Charles J. Connick Associates.

Our Chapel windows are different from ordinary windows; for when we look at an ordinary window, we see through it that which is within range of our vision; but when we look at these windows, we are not looking through clear glass, neither do we see merely glass that has been colored by the infusion of metallic oxides into it, or by the burning of pigments into its surface. We see something more even than Milton's

"Storied windows richly dight,
Casting a dim religious light."

In the aisle windows, for instance, we saw not the beautiful stained glass only, but also historic doorways and historic towers. And when we look into these clerestory windows, we have a vision of greatness: persons of great aims, great virtues, and great achievements. If Whitehead is correct in opining that "the sense of greatness is the groundwork of morals," then these windows should furnish the groundwork of morals for those who view them with any swift sensitiveness to greatness.

Great persons are presented in the following order, — starting at the balcony, and reading counterclockwise; that is, from right to left, on the east side of the chapel:

Abraham. The medallion at the bottom depicts Abraham about to sacrifice Isaac, and prevented by the angel.

Moses. The medallion shows him before the burning bush.

Elijah. The medallion represents him at Mount Carmel.

Isaiah. The medallion depicts the cherubim touching Isaiah's lips with the burning coal.

[86]

John the Baptist, whose medallion portrays the baptism of Jesus.

Peter, whose medallion shows him preaching at Pentecost and the tongues of fire on the heads of the Apostles.

Paul. The medallion represents the Damascus road conversion experience.

John. The medallion delineates the Disciples at the Last Supper with Jesus, and features the Beloved Disciple.

On the west side, beginning at the chancel, and reading from right to left toward the balcony, eight dynamic personalities are represented, as follows:

Athanasius, with a medallion which shows him riding a donkey as he returns from exile, a multitude greeting him.

Augustine, whose medallion shows him in the garden with Monica, his mother.

Saint Francis of Assisi, who in the medallion is casting down his garments of opulence and announcing his quest for poverty.

Martin Luther, whose medallion shows him in the Diet of Worms, taking his stand before the Emperor.

John Wesley. The medallion depicts him preaching to the multitude from a position on top of his father's tombstone.

Francis Asbury, who is seen, in the medallion, on horseback.

Abraham Lincoln, beneath whose towering form is a medallion showing him freeing a slave.

Frances E. Willard. The medallion portrays her presenting to President Grover Cleveland the Polyglot Petition with seven million signatures.

In the pages that follow, let us refresh our knowledge of these worthies, lingering with each one a little while. As we gaze upon them, and read the brief sketches which I have written, our imaginations will add in the background many dazzling episodes and heroic achievements and epochal movements in the Near East and Rome and Germany and England and America. If our sense of greatness is an immediate intuition, then the following pages should be an inspiration to action and to moral progress.

Abraham

ABRAHAM was a traveler. We read that he "went down into Egypt"; "he went up out of Egypt"; "he dwelt in the land of Canaan"; "he came and dwelt in the plain," and so the story runs. He has been described as a cosmopolitan.

Abraham went forth under the conviction that he was called by God: "The Lord said unto Abraham." He was moved by hidden influences. He had a sense of destiny upon him. He had heard God say: "I will make thee a great nation, and I will bless thee." Abraham was driven on by the enthusiasm of a great cause. Away he went from Ur of the Chaldees, carrying his culture as a gift of God to be bestowed on others. He was as much of an internationalist as he was the father of a nation.

Believing God, he went upward and onward, lured forward by a great promise and a great faith. His line of march was marked by altars, evidence of the worship that sustained his faith: "And there he builded an altar unto the Lord."

Abraham was tested. He was tested by poverty and famine, by worldly policy, and by the choice of worldly possession. His supreme test is described with tragic force, and is full of profound pathos, the demand, according to the practice of the time, to sacrifice his only son, Isaac. It was the testing of his faith. But his faith and his filial obedience made forever luminous the Divine words that "to obey is better than sacrifice." Written in gold also are the words: "Abraham believed God, and it was counted to him for righteousness."

A window representing Abraham is appropriate in the Chapel. He was "a friend of God." He was a cosmopolitan at the beginning, but a God-centered individual at the end. His vision, his courage, and his faith guided him to the tomorrow of life and of history.

[88]

ABRAHAM

"By faith Abraham, when he was called, obeyed; and he went out, not knowing whither he went. . . . He looked for a city which hath foundations, whose builder and maker is God."

Moses

MOSES was the dynamic character of the exodus, the going out of Israel from the land of night to the land of light, from the land of bondage to the Promised Land. Moses was a multifaceted personality, having aptitudes for new tasks, and facility in various fields of service.

Moses was the motive force of Jewish liberation: a natural-born leader of men, with vision and courage, and a certain audacity that made him invincible when he believed himself to be right. He was the emancipator of a horde of Hebrew slaves. He was a discoverer and explorer of the way to the Promised Land. He was a practical builder, building the tabernacle, a legal system of government, and a ritual for the religious worship of Israel.

Moses was a law-giver: the Ten Commandments are planetary in their significance; they are a universal law, timely and timeless. He was a humanitarian: there is nothing local or national about his service to mankind. He was a cosmopolite: even his grave was never localized. He was a natural-born preacher.

Moses was a religious leader who inaugurated or promulgated the idea that the common life may be religious. He was an opener of eyes: he saw the Divine nimbus that rests over the commonplace.

All the foregoing descriptions may accurately be made of Moses, but the best description of him is in five words found in First Chronicles 23:14: *"Moses the man of God."* This explains everything else that was great about him. He was also a man of prayer. He was on terms of intimate communion with God. His face took on an unconscious beauty because of his fellowship with the Most High.

While Moses lived, he lived with God; he did his work as in the constant presence of God, and when he died, he died in God's company.

MOSES

"By faith Moses forsook
Egypt, not fearing the
wrath of the king; for he
endured, as seeing Him
who is invisible."

Elijah

ELIJAH burst unannounced upon the stage of life. He played a leading part in the drama of his times. The scenery in the foreground changed with each act and with each scene; but the scenery in the background remained the same. Great personalities moved upon the stage — King Ahab, Queen Jezebel, the prophets of Baal, the King's messengers, the multitudinous people. Elijah constantly dominated the drama.

The first act shows the land of Israel filled with idolatry. Then comes Elijah, stern, bleak, grand, majestic, awe-inspiring, denouncing the wickedness of the court and the idolatry of the land, and predicting vengeance, drought, and famine.

The next act opens with Elijah summoning the people to a decision: "How long halt ye between two opinions? If the Lord be God, follow Him: but if Baal, then follow him. And the people answered him not a word." Then on Mount Carmel, Elijah sets the stage for the manifestation of Jehovah's power. The test is to be by fire, and Lo! the fire descends, and the people shout, "The Lord, He is God! The Lord, He is God!"

Then comes the third dramatic and colorful episode. Elijah flees to Mount Horeb, and there this impulsive man gives way to a feeling of depression. He can conceive of no way for the triumph of righteousness except through physical force and violence. While crouching in his cave, a hurricane breaks loose. The juniper trees are tossed and uprooted. The hurricane is followed by an earthquake, which makes the mountain tremble like a frightened child. The earthquake is followed by a fire, — sheet lightning and forked lightning! But Elijah finds no answer in earthquake, wind, or fire, but in the soft stillness that follows, as he looks out across the desert, he hears the Voice — the still small Voice — speaking to his soul.

ELIJAH

"Elijah came unto all the people, and said, How long halt ye between two opinions? if the Lord be God, follow Him!"

Isaiah

ISAIAH was the greatest of the Hebrew prophets. His personality was both smashing and winsome, magnetic and compelling. He was the foremost politician and statesman of his generation. His statesmanship was marked by patience, courage, and wisdom. His ministry was long, at least thirty-nine years, from "the year that King Uzziah died" (B.C. 740) to the year of the deliverance of Jerusalem from Sennacherib (B.C. 701). His literary style is simple and sublime, tender and bold. He exerted upon subsequent prophecy an influence that was both strong and determinative.

Isaiah was a citizen of Jerusalem, with constant access to the court and presence of the King. Jerusalem holds his past and his future; his ambition and his aspiration; his love and his paradise. He acquaints us with its streets, the fashions of its women, with the arrival of embassies, with the rumors that pass through it, with its profligacies and its afflictions: war, siege, famine, pestilence, earthquake, turbulence, panic, triumph, and worship.

Isaiah started his ministry with a vision of holiness and a sense of call. He beheld a transforming vision in the Temple, and heard words that influenced his whole life: "Holy, holy, holy, is the Lord of hosts: the whole earth is full of His glory." He had a sense of his own sinfulness, and asked for cleansing, whereupon his lips were touched with a live coal from off the altar. Then when he heard God asking whom He might send, Isaiah answered, "Here am I, send me." From then on, prayer and preaching, reform and statesmanship were blent in his career like carillonic bells. He preached both the majestic transcendence of God and the universality of God throughout "the whole earth." "Holy, holy, holy, is the Lord of hosts: the earth is full of His glory."

ISAIAH

"I heard the voice of the Lord, saying, Whom shall I send, and who will go for us? Then said I, Here am I: send me!"

John the Baptist

JOHN THE BAPTIST was one of the most striking personages in Bible history. He fulfilled within himself the prophecy of Isaiah: "The voice of him that crieth in the wilderness, Prepare ye the way of the Lord, make straight in the desert a highway for our God."

At about thirty years of age, he entered upon his ministry of revivalism and reform, which he carried on partly in the Desert of Judea, and partly in the Jordan Valley. He was a strange, weird figure, dressed in the rough raiment of the hills. From the solitudes of the wilderness, he came preaching and baptizing. He announced the near approach of the Kingdom of Heaven, demanding moral preparation for it.

John the Baptist was a prophetic voice. His mission was uncompromising. The intensity and the passion of his message can be sensed from the words he used, such words as "Repent," "Prepare," "the Ax at the root of the tree," "Purge the floor," "Burn the chaff," "Wrath to come," "Generation of vipers." But note that over against this scathing denunciation of the wickedness of the day, John spoke the tenderest words that human lips could frame. They were words concerning Jesus: "Behold the Lamb of God, which taketh away the sin of the world."

John showed his sense of proportion by a frank and honest statement that Jesus was greater than he; that Jesus must increase while he must decrease.

Jesus esteemed John highly, declaring that he was "more than a prophet": that he was "a burning and a shining light."

John the Baptist was like some high and rocky peak that was colored red with the approach of dawn; but which was softened, subdued, and overcome by the sun whose rising it had foretold.

[96]

JOHN THE
BAPTIST

"My joy therefore is ful-
filled. He must increase,
but I must decrease."

Peter

PETER was a vacillating and impetuous man; now timid, now bold; now cowardly, now courageous; now impulsive, now steady; always prone to err, always quick to repent.

One of the most striking episodes in his career took place at Caesarea Philippi. Jesus had taken His followers to this beautiful retreat to prepare both Himself and them for the approaching crisis which He clearly foresaw. Jesus asked His Disciples for their appraisement of Him. Peter, in a luminous moment of inspiration and enthusiasm, blurted out a memorable utterance in which he revealed a profound knowledge of the nature of Jesus: "Thou art the Christ, the Son of the living God." Jesus was pleased with His ardent Disciple's prompt and unwavering devotion. Then, making symbolic use of the surname (a "stone") which He had bestowed upon Peter, He eulogized him, speaking in words so obviously figurative and emotional that they can be twisted into meaning almost anything that a partisan wishes them to mean: "Thou art Peter, and upon this rock I will build my church. . . . I will give unto thee the keys of the Kingdom of Heaven."

Whatever else these words may mean, one thing is certain: Jesus, who had combatted the priestcraft of His day even unto death, did not intend to build up a new priestcraft more dominant than the old. Origen, one of the Church fathers, insists that the promise was made not to Peter alone but to every disciple who joins in Peter's confession. Saint Chrysostom holds that the *rock* was not Peter but Peter's faith, "the faith of his confession."

Peter slept in Gethsemane when Jesus longed for his sympathy, and cursed and swore that he did not know Jesus when Jesus was on trial. But after the Resurrection, Jesus met Peter on the shore of Galilee, and restored him, commanding him to feed His sheep and His lambs.

[98]

SAINT PETER

"Then Simon Peter answered Him: Lord, to whom shall we go? Thou hast the words of eternal life."

Paul

SAUL of Tarsus was no mediocre man. Out of the line of his ancestry had come the first King of Israel. His father was a citizen of the Roman Empire, which meant that Saul was a freeborn citizen of Rome. He was a Pharisee of the Pharisees, the strictest sect of the Jews. He had been educated at the University of Tarsus. He studied at the feet of Professor Gamaliel, in Jerusalem. He was trained to be a rabbi, and evidently looked forward to sitting in the temple porch, with a group of disciples about him, who would follow with reverence his teaching.

As a member of the Sanhedrin, his social position was established. In that august body, he had voted vengeance upon the followers of Jesus. He stood by and held the coats of certain assailants who stoned Stephen to death. He secured authority to proceed as far as Damascus, wreaking still greater vengeance upon the Christians.

Then came his life-transforming experience on the road to Damascus. He passed through a change which, according to his own appraisement, was equal to that of creation in its emergence from chaos. He ever after contended that he had seen the living Jesus in that experience. All the rest of his life was built upon that conviction.

He now received the new name of Paul, and became an apostle of the Lord whose followers he had persecuted. He traveled everywhere, toiling day and night, suffering privation for those who did not even thank him. He was ship-wrecked, and stoned, and beaten with many stripes. He finally had his head cut off on the block in Rome. He literally gave himself for persons who were living without God and without hope in the world.

John

OHN's father, Zebedee, was a fisherman on the Sea of Galilee.
John was a member of his company. Evidently the father was
well-to-do, for he had a number of hired helpers. John's mother was
a sister of Mary, the mother of Jesus.

John was well-born, and socially well-placed. Not only was his
father one of the more prosperous members of his community, but
both his father and mother were well regarded in their religious
fellowship. The social standing of the family is indicated by the
fact that John was acquainted with Caiaphas, the High Priest, —
and that was a sort of "Social Register" of that day.

By nature, John was a man of high temper. Jesus once playfully
described him as a "son of thunder." His mother believed in him,
and was ambitious for him, and John was not lacking ambition in
himself. When first we meet John, he is full of fire, and ready to
make appeal to physical force and violence. He wanted to call down
fire upon persons who blocked his way, or with whom he did not
agree. He desired the chief place in the Kingdom of God, and his
mother aided and abetted him in this lofty ambition.

But John followed Jesus, and learned of Him. He submitted
himself to the wonder-working, transforming power of Jesus. He
still remained a personality and a man of character, but how different! He was one of the three Disciples — Peter, James and John
— most closely linked to Christ in heart and life. He was taken into
the most intimate fellowship with Jesus. He seemed to have a
profounder and truer understanding of the Saviour than any other
of His Disciples. He was the one who leaned upon Jesus' bosom
at the Last Supper. He was with Him in Gethsemane. He went with
Him into the High Priest's court during the trial. He was at the foot
of the cross during the crucifixion, and then he took the mother of
Jesus home with him.

SAINT JOHN

"The Word was made flesh, and dwelt among us (and we beheld His glory, the glory as of the only begotten of the Father,) full of grace and truth."

Athanasius

ATHANASIUS was born in Alexandria in 296 or 298 A.D. His was a period of religious and political conflict, hatred, hostility, persecution. Under Constantine, Christianity had become a state religion, with the result that much of the Church's life had become secularized. The natural result was an intellectual internal war.

Even as a child, Athanasius displayed unusual qualities of leadership and of mental agility, and powers of penetration and analysis. He was at home with Greek literature and Greek philosophy, and studied most diligently the Bible.

The rise of Aryanism meant dissension in the Church. The Council of Nicaea was called. Athanasius was the hero of the Council in his opposition to Aryanism. His eloquence and zeal made him a marked man.

Athanasius was made a bishop when only thirty years of age. He became one of the most powerful ecclesiastics in the world. He came into conflict with the emperor. He was lied about, maligned, physically beaten and exiled. In fact, he was exiled five different times.

Athanasius was a great Christian and a great theologian. At the same time, he was a man of pronounced resourcefulness. He was both practical and liberal. He was brave and upright.

He waged a valiant fight for the deity of our Lord. It is easy to believe that the clear and keen intellect of Athanasius helped to preserve a doctrine which found expression more than sixteen hundred years later in beautiful hymn written by a graduate of Boston University, Harry Webb Farrington:

> "I know not how that Bethlehem's Babe
> Could in the God-head be;
> I only know the manger Child
> Has brought God's life to me."

SAINT ATHANASIUS

"How would men become Christians, or the Church abide, if there were no pastors?"

Saint Augustine

SAINT AUGUSTINE was born at Tagaste, in northern Africa, in 354 A.D. He was of pure Roman blood. As a boy Augustine lived a selfish, wicked life. Growing to manhood, he studied until he mastered Latin literature, rhetoric, logic, and philosophy. But he plunged into gross licentiousness; believed continence to be impossible, and lived a life of libertinism.

Monica, his mother, was praying and working for his conversion. His restlessness led him inevitably to Rome, but instead of finding peace, he found only new disappointments and disillusionments. Then he went to Milan to teach rhetoric. At Milan he became acquainted with Bishop Ambrose, whom he "heard with pleasure." All the time his sense of sin was deepening, and his need of God and God's forgiveness was increasing.

One afternoon, he went "into the garden," and while he walked there he asked himself the question whose answer he had been seeking: "How long, tomorrow and tomorrow? Why is there not this hour an end to my uncleanness?" Then while he was weeping in "bitter contrition of heart," he "heard from a neighboring house a voice, as of boy or girl, I know not, chanting and oft repeating, *'Tolle, lege,'* 'Take up and read.' " It seemed to him like "a voice from heaven." He returned to the house, took up a volume of Saint Paul's Epistles, opened it and read the words that first met his eyes: "Not in rioting and drunkenness, not in chambering and wantonness, not in strife and envying: but put ye on the Lord Jesus Christ, and make not provision for the flesh to fulfill the lusts thereof."

As he finished reading "all the darkness of doubt vanished away." He at last had "found rest for his soul." God had "waked in man."

The story is simply told from there on. He was baptized, joined the church, started out on a religious career, was soon made Bishop of Hippo Regius, where he labored faithfully to the end of his life.

SAINT AUGUSTINE

"Thou hast made us for
Thyself, and our hearts
are restless till they rest
in Thee."

Saint Francis of Assisi

FRANCESCO, son of Peter Bernadone, was born at Assisi, Italy, about 1181 A.D. His education was slight and inconsequential. He spent his youth in frivolity. When twenty-one years of age, he gave a banquet to his friends. They had a roistering time, and crowned Francis king of the revelers. His friends found him later in a trance. It was the crisis in his life. From that moment he was a changed man.

He spent much time in solitude, in prayer, and in service to the poor. His father contemplated the expansion of his financial empire by a rich marriage for Francis. When Francis rebelled, the father sought to bring pressure upon him by taking him to a church court. When Francis insisted that he would continue his charities, the father threatened to disinherit him. Whereupon Francis took off his rich raiment and flung it on the ground at his father's feet, and handed back to him his wallet, and declared that henceforth he would be married to Lady Poverty. He espoused poverty, but not mendicancy. He was a mystic, a poet, a preacher, an inspirer. He composed the following prayer which we might wisely pray and live:

> "Lord, make me an instrument of Thy Peace!
> Where there is hatred . . . let me sow love
> Where there is injury . . . pardon
> Where there is doubt . . . faith
> Where there is despair . . . hope
> Where there is sadness . . . joy!
> O Divine Master, grant that I may not so much seek
> To be consoled . . . as to console
> To be understood . . . as to understand
> To be loved . . . as to love, for
> It is in giving . . . that we receive
> It is in pardoning . . . that we are pardoned
> It is in dying . . . that we are born to eternal life."

SAINT FRANCIS
OF ASSISI

"It becomes us, by the
example of Christ, rather
to do than to teach, and
to do and teach together."

Martin Luther

"THE Catholic Church in the opening years of the sixteenth century . . . was grievously sick in head and in members," so
declares a distinguished Roman Catholic historian. "Even the best
of physicians would scarcely have known where to begin the cure.
And then there appeared . . . a personality of genius. This was
Martin Luther." *

Martin Luther was the son of a German coal miner. He begged
and sang his way through the preparatory schools. He graduated
from the University of Erfurt, at that time the most renowned University in Germany. Then he entered the convent of the Augustinian
Friars, and became a monk — and he was a model of monkish piety.
He spent four weeks in what he called "Holy Rome." He climbed
on his knees the twenty-eight steps of the Scala Sancta. He became a
professor in Wittenberg University. A life of honor and ease and
influence in the Church of Rome was opening before him. Yet he
turned aside from it all, and, with the grip of ungloved earnestness,
he seized western Europe by the rims, and shook it and shook it till
he shook its history from unconsciousness into reality. He shook it
till he awakened the moral indignation of the peasants. He shook it
till he aroused the sleeping conscience of the leaders. He shook it
till the rafters of the house of tradition rattled. He shook it till he
shook ignorance out of education, and superstition out of religion.
He shook it till the flinty rocks of truth emitted sparks that kindled
the fires of justification by faith throughout all the world. (?)

He ended his speech in the climactic Diet of Worms with the
fateful words: "I am bound by the Scriptures; . . . I may not, and
will not, recant, because to act against conscience is unholy and
unsafe. So help me God! Amen."

* Hughes: A POPULAR HISTORY OF THE CATHOLIC CHURCH, p. 156.
Copyright 1947 by the Macmillan Company and used with their permission. This
book has the censor's "nihil obstat," and the vicar general's "imprimatur."

[110] *Protestant viewpoint on Luther.*

MARTIN LUTHER

"Here I stand. I can do no other. God help me!"

John Wesley

NARROWNESS, bigotry, and intolerance had no place in John Wesley's words or work. Let him speak for himself: "I beseech you, brethren, by the mercies of God, that we be in no wise divided among ourselves. Is thy heart right, as my heart is with thine? I ask no further question. If it be, give me thine hand. For opinions, or terms, let us not destroy the work of God. Dost thou love and serve God? It is enough. I give thee the right hand of fellowship."

His followers were called "Methodists." The term was at first derisive, but because of the quality of lives lived by its followers, it became a term of honor. Let Wesley give us his definition of a Methodist:

"A Methodist is one who lives according to the method laid down in the Bible.

"He is one who loves the Lord with all his heart, who prays without ceasing and in everything gives thanks. His heart is full of love to all mankind, and is purified from envy, malice, wrath and every unkind affection.

"He keeps all God's commandments from the least unto the greatest. He follows not the customs of the world. He cannot speak evil of his neighbor any more than he can lie. He does good unto all men, neighbors, friends and enemies.

"These are the principles and practices of our sect. These are the marks of a true Methodist. By these alone, do Methodists desire to be distinguished from other men."

Who today — of whatever faith — would not be glad to have those words describe his life and practice? With the Quaker poet we pray:

"O Lord and Master of us all:
What'er our name or sign,
We own Thy sway, we hear Thy call,
We test our lives by Thine!"

JOHN WESLEY

"I look upon all the
world as my parish."

Francis Asbury

FRANCIS ASBURY was the type and flower of the Methodist circuit riders whom Theodore Roosevelt credits with stirring the fearless backwoodsmen "to the depths of their natures," and transforming them into "strong and helpful props of the communities whose foundations they helped to lay."

Francis Asbury, elected Bishop at the memorable Christmas Conference of 1784, gave dynamic leadership to the movement that saw Methodist preachers in almost every wagon train of pioneers who took the trail to the wilderness.

During his ministry, Asbury traveled on horseback a total of 275,000 miles on the wilderness trail, through malaria-ridden swamps, from one settlement to another. He traveled on through heat and cold, through drenching rain and driving snow — he traveled on with sore throat, aching head, burning with fever. He drove his frail body on and on, from Maine to Georgia, from New York to Tennessee, from the wilderness of Kentucky to New England. He preached some 16,500 sermons. Starting out without much formal education, he read diligently and discriminately. His saddle was his study, and his saddle bags his library. He became a good scholar, the peer of any American of his day. He was a profound Bible student, with a complete mastery of the Greek and Hebrew languages. He was a man of prayer. As an administrator, he excelled, bringing order out of a chaotic condition in an infant church and on a godless frontier.

Asbury died in 1816, after fifty-five years in the ministry, forty-five of which were spent in America. At his death, it was said that more Americans had seen his face than the face of any other person.

A statue of Asbury on horseback stands at an important street intersection in the national capital of the country whose moral foundations Asbury so valiantly helped to lay.

[114]

FRANCIS ASBURY

"I go to live with God,
and to teach others so to
do."

Abraham Lincoln

BRAHAM LINCOLN was the Saviour of the American Union and the emancipator of four million slaves.

If anyone ever fulfilled Browning's dictum that "a man's reach should exceed his grasp," it was Abraham Lincoln. It was a long reach from the backwoods cabin in Kentucky, where he was born, to the White House in Washington, where he died. It was a long reach from the boy that lay upon the puncheon floor of a frontier cabin, writing with a piece of charcoal on the back of a wooden shovel by the flickering light of a pine knot, to the man who wrote the Gettysburg Address and the Second Inaugural. Lincoln had "no form nor comeliness," and in him there was "no beauty that we should desire him," but he had a beautiful soul. He was lean and lank and tall; but his mind was higher than his body. His hands and feet were ungainly and big, but Lilliputian by comparison with his heart. His eyes were deep-set as though the knuckles of sorrow had pushed them back into their sockets.

He was tolerant, but firm in his convictions. He was kind and unselfish. He was magnanimous and forgiving. He had an unshakable faith in God and in His overruling Providence. The Scriptural cadences of his speeches were freighted with a moral intensity. "The Almighty has His own purposes," he declared in his Second Inaugural. Affirming and reaffirming his faith in the justice of his cause and in the righteousness of God, he concludes his brief Second Inaugural with a sentence that is one of the noblest utterances in the whole world of literature: "With malice toward none, with charity for all, with firmness in the right as God gives us to see the right, let us strive on to finish the work we are in, to bind up the nation's wounds, to care for him who shall have borne the battle and for his widow and his orphans, to do all which may achieve and cherish a just and a lasting peace among ourselves and with all nations."

ABRAHAM LINCOLN

"This nation, under God, shall have a new birth of freedom."

Frances E. Willard

I DARE to prophesy, that as the years go by, and the history of the New World comes to be read by those who desire to know the builders that reared a civilization so great and so strong, the name of Frances Willard will stand by the side of Lincoln, Wendell Phillips and Garrison," so declared Lady Henry Somerset, of England.

Frances Elizabeth Willard was born in 1839, and died in 1898. When she was seven years of age, her family moved by prairie schooner to Wisconsin. We view her favorably as a public school and college teacher, as a traveler abroad, and as professor of aesthetics and Dean of Women at Northwestern University.

While she was a college student, Miss Willard was religiously awakened, and joined the Methodist Church. Her upbringing, her religious convictions, her natural bent for reform, all combined to put her into the temperance movement. She became the inspiration of the movement for total abstinence and temperance reform. Lady Somerset called her "the greatest woman philanthropist of our generation."

Not only was Miss Willard the President of the National Women's Christian Temperance Union, but she was also the Founder and the first President of the World's Woman's Christian Temperance Union. Her ability as a leader and organizer is illustrated by the fact that under her generalship a Polyglot Petition was circulated among the nations of the world. This Petition, with seven million signatures, Miss Willard presented to President Grover Cleveland in the White House.

A statue of Frances E. Willard stands among the nation's heroes in the rotunda of the Capitol at Washington, the only woman in that greatest of all halls of fame. It is a monument to a beautiful life.

FRANCES E. WILLARD

"The struggle of the soul
is toward expression."

Balcony Windows

THE window at the end of the balcony *on the east side* of the Chapel is composed of two lancets of four medallions each. The eight persons pictured are all religious men, and all educators of outstanding importance in their respective eras and fields.

The four in the left-hand lancet are world figures, forever famous as pioneers in great movements, — Erasmus, Comenius, Horace Mann, and Booker T. Washington. Each one's work was epochal in its vast significance and importance.

The four medallions in the right-hand lancet are all Boston University men, the first two (reading from bottom to top) being members of the faculty, and the second two, alumni of Boston University. Professor Borden Parker Bowne is representative of the humanities and liberal culture, and Professor Alexander Graham Bell is representative of scientific research and invention.

The third one, Francis J. McConnell, would rate a place in any Chapel because of his contributions to religious thought and humane progress, and would rate a place in any university hall because of the excellence of his educational achievements.

The top medallion contains four figures. The one on the left is George L. Fox, a graduate of Boston University. Read, on the following pages, why he is there, and then be grateful for the tolerance that bound him and his Protestant, Roman Catholic and Jewish comrades together in death, but despise the bigotry that keeps their successors apart in life.

The window at the end of the balcony *on the western side* of the Chapel also consists of two lancets, containing four medallions each. The left-hand lancet has pictures of four great Deans of the oldest School of Boston University. They are not the only Deans worthy of such recognition; but they stand out in such vital relation to our history that they become representatives of all. Reading from top

[120]

to bottom: Osmon C. Baker was the first head of the infant School of Theology when it was located at Newbury, Vermont. John Dempster was the second titular head, and at the same time the man whose faith, indefatigable labor and devotion saved the School. James E. Latimer would rate a place here on a twofold count: both because he was the first Dean of the School after it was incorporated into Boston University, and second, because of his profound scholarship. Albert C. Knudson stands as a type of the best of which the School can boast in modern history, and was one of the inspiring teachers of both the present Dean and also of the present President.

In the right-hand lancet, the four medallions are of the only four Presidents the University has had since it was chartered under its present name. Reading from top to bottom: William Fairfield Warren, the informing genius of the University and President from 1873 until 1903; William E. Huntington, from 1904 to 1911; Lemuel H. Murlin, from 1911 to 1925, and Daniel L. Marsh since the 1st of February, 1926.

I accept full personal responsibility for the personages selected to go into these windows. When I was planning for the lancet dedicated to the Presidents, I had in mind placing in the window only the first three Presidents; but certain advisers of mine were so insistent that the pictured presidential roster should be complete up to date that I yielded, believing that there might be more of vanity — or mock modesty — in omitting the last one than in including it.

These four men have marched in the van of the University's progress, — progress from littleness to bigness, but retaining all the value of the little while adding the value of the big; the march from the provincial to the cosmopolitan, but losing no loyalties in the process; the march from separate and second-hand housing to a unified campus of modern and adequate buildings; the march from the denominational to the ecumenical, but keeping alive all the while the spiritual glow.

All the characters presented in these medallions will be discussed in the following pages.

Erasmus

ERASMUS was born in 1466, out of wedlock, — his mother was the talented daughter of a physician; his father, an artist who later became a priest. Dishonest guardians thrust Erasmus, in his teens, into a monastery, trying to force him into becoming a monk. He rebelled; left the monastery; earned his living by teaching; worked his way up to such learning as the University of Paris could give. Wanting to master Greek, he went to Oxford, where he came under the influence of Colet, and caught his fervor for reform.

On the accession of Henry VIII of England, the hopes of the Oxford students rose. Erasmus, who had been traveling on the continent, came back to London, and there wrote his *Praise of Folly,* a satire on the follies of the age, particularly on the scholastic theologians.

Erasmus tried to be neutral in the Luther-Roman Catholic conflict; but when asked by the Elector of Saxony "what he really thought of Luther," Erasmus replied, with a smile, "Luther has committed two crimes! He has hit the Pope on the crown and the monks on the belly." However, Erasmus held aloof from the struggle, urging moderation on both sides, preaching unity, and going on with his own works, chief of which was his edition of the New Testament. It is the verdict of history that nothing else so paved the way for the Protestant Reformation as that great work.

In spite of persecutions and counter persecutions, toleration was one of the by-products of the Protestant revolution, and the works of Erasmus did much to prepare the minds of men for its ultimate adoption.

Erasmus was the most broadly educated man of his time, and the most perfect exponent of humanism which his age supplied. At the close of the fifteenth century it was said: "Whatever is artistic, finished, learned and wise is called Erasmian."

Comenius

JOHN AMOS COMENIUS has a double claim upon a memorial in this Chapel. As a great religious leader, he merits a place in any chapel or church, and as "the greatest of all pedagogues," he deserves to be honored in any university's most important building.

Comenius was born at Nivnitz, Moravia, in 1592. He was educated chiefly at Herborn and Heidelberg, and traveled widely throughout England, and the rest of Europe.

He was brought up in the faith of the Moravian and Bohemian Brethren, a Denomination that stressed devotional religious experience. He was ordained a preacher in his Church, and rose to the influential rank of a bishop.

But it is as the father of modern education that Comenius is best known. He began to teach at twenty-two years of age. He was disgusted with the pedantic teaching of that day. It was formal and lifeless, killed by the effects of medievalism, and entombed by the heavy hand of the authority of the past.

He wrote voluminously. In his *The Great Didactic* he founded the modern science of pedagogy. His epochal work, *The World Illustrated,* was the first illustrated textbook ever written, and was the beginning of modern methods of object teaching. His book, *The Gate of Tongues Unlocked,* completely changed the method of teaching languages, and was translated into nearly all the languages of Europe and several of those of Asia.

Comenius believed that the proper end of education was fitness for the Kingdom of God. He considered children as immortal beings with a supernatural character which, while it should never be lost to sight, is to be carefully studied in its analogy to the whole order of nature.

Comenius's work as a whole shows an intellect above the limitations of his own or any other century.

[124]

Horace Mann

HORACE MANN was born at Franklin, Massachusetts, in 1796. In boyhood and youth, he worked on a farm and attended the public schools. When twenty years of age, he began the study of Latin and Greek, and prepared himself privately to enter the junior year of Brown University. After graduation, he studied law.

In 1837, Horace Mann was made Executive Secretary of the Massachusetts Board of Education, which position he held for twelve years. He completely reformed the public school system, and lifted it to a higher level. "In a Republic, ignorance is a crime," he thundered. His most memorable achievement was the establishment, in 1837, of a normal school system which we now call teachers' colleges, — the first in the United States. He was the pioneer of professional training for teachers.

Horace Mann is a good illustration of the creative power of a new idea as well as of the "expulsive power of a new affection." Before he was made Secretary of the Board of Education, he was in no sense a professional educator. He was a lawyer, with a humanitarian bent and an interest in statesmanship. The turning point in his career came when he was made Secretary of the Board of Education, which had just been created. His appointment was significant for education and Democracy, and at the same time for Mann himself. His new job was the spark that exploded the sleeping explosives in his mind, and blasted out a new work for him which led to immortal renown.

Having finished his epochal work in Massachusetts, and after a brief service in Congress, he became President of Antioch College, in Ohio. Near the end of his distinguished career, in 1859, he delivered a commencement address, the closing sentence of which is worthy of all acceptation: "Be ashamed to die until you have won some victory for humanity."

Booker T. Washington

BOOKER T. WASHINGTON was a man sent of God, the foremost American Negro of our national history. He was a loyal American; an educator-statesman, and a man with a purpose dedicated to the welfare of the Negro.

He was born (about 1859) into slavery on a plantation in Franklin County, Virginia. As he described it, he was "a slave among slaves," until he was freed by Lincoln. He never knew who his father was. In youth he went to West Virginia, where he worked in a salt furnace and in a coal mine, and as a house servant. He obtained elementary education by studying at night. When thirteen years of age, he walked the five hundred miles to Hampton Institute. He was a student there for three years, paying his way by working as a janitor.

In 1881 he was appointed organizer and principal of a Negro normal School at Tuskegee, Alabama. The place in which he established his school was "a rather dilapidated shanty near the Colored Methodist Church, together with the church itself as a sort of assembly room." From that humble beginning, the world-famous Tuskegee Normal and Industrial Institute has been developed. Its growth is due largely to consecration and the good common sense of Booker T. Washington. He laid special emphasis upon the industrial education of Negroes. He was convinced that it was only as they gained economic independence that they could better their conditions.

In his autobiography, Washington calls attention to the fact that while stress has been laid upon the industrial side of the work at Tuskegee, yet "we do not neglect or overlook in any degree the religious and spiritual side. The school is strictly undenominational, but it is thoroughly Christian, and the spiritual training of the students is not neglected."

[128]

BOOKER T. WASHINGTON

Borden Parker Bowne

ORDEN PARKER BOWNE was "distinctly America's first philosopher." So declared Rudolf Eucken, Nobel prize winning
German philosopher of Jena. Similar appraisement can be quoted
from many other competent European critics.

Bowne was born of industrious and God-fearing parents, in Leon-
ardville, New Jersey, in 1847. Graduating from New York Univer-
sity with highest honors, he decided to enter the ministry of the
Methodist Church, and was ordained by the great Bishop Matthew
Simpson. After a year's experience in the pastorate, he studied in
Europe, at Paris, Halle, and Gottingen.

In 1876, he was appointed Professor of Philosophy at Boston
University, where he remained until the day of his death in 1910, —
thirty-four years as Professor of Philosophy and Dean of the Graduate School. He believed that philosophy had a mission to everyday
living. Rigorous logician though he was, yet he made "the field of
life and action" his supreme court of appeal as against the "arid
wastes of formal logic."

Bowne described himself as a "theistic idealist." "Personalism"
is the distinctive name for his system of philosophy. The reality and
character of the Infinite Person received his greatest emphasis. He
saw in theism "the supreme condition of both thought and life."
Without a theistic faith, "we must stand as dumb and hopeless before the deeper questions of thought and life as a Papuan or a
Patagonian before an eclipse."

Bowne was a great and stimulating teacher. His literary style
was clear, concise, and compact. Epigrammatic sayings sparkle on
every page of his profound philosophical writings. He loved the
true: pursuit of it was his life quest. He loved the good, and personalized it. He loved the beautiful also, and enjoyed it in his home,
in his library, and in his famous rose garden.

[130]

BORDEN PARKER BOWNE

Alexander Graham Bell

ALEXANDER GRAHAM BELL was born in Edinburgh, Scotland, in 1847. In 1873, he was appointed Professor of Speech in Boston University. Forty-three years later, he said at a reception tendered him in Boston: "It was while I was connected with Boston University that all the work was done on the telephone."

On the 20th of October, 1874, he wrote to his parents: "I am tonight a happy man. Success seems to meet me on every hand. First, pupils pour in. Second, the medical society has evinced great interest in the ear experiments."

These "ear experiments" were precursors of his work on the telephone. By his study of the possibility of telegraphing musical notes, he captured the principle of the telephone. On the 18th of March, 1875, he secured from President Warren permission to "put off all classes until the 12th of April." He was working frantically now upon his invention. He needed both time and money. Therefore, President Warren advanced him his salary for the next year's work. "Without this aid," said Bell later, "I would not have been able to get along at all."

He had his wires strung around his classroom in Boston University. He was working during the day in his classroom, and at night in his little shop. In a synopsis of telephone chronology, Bell records: "First telephone constructed, and speech-sounds heard, June, 1875."

Then came the Centennial Exposition in Philadelphia, 1876. Bell exhibited his invention. The attention given to it by the most feted guest of honor, Don Pedro, Emperor of Brazil, attracted to it wide attention. Bell was given the Grand Award.

In 1889, at the time of the Paris World's Fair, Boston University was given the gold medal for Professor Bell's invention.

Professor Alexander Graham Bell was a benefactor of mankind.

Francis J. McConnell

FRANCIS JOHN McCONNELL was born in Trinway, Ohio, on the 18th of August in 1871. We are glad that he is still alive at the time of this writing. His father was a Methodist preacher in Ohio and in New England. His mother was a gracious and kindly woman, combining within her personality deep religious devotion and shrewd practicalities.

Francis J. McConnell did his graduate work in Boston University, where he earned three degrees — S.T.B., A.M., and Ph.D. He was later awarded a number of honorary degrees, Boston University conferring upon him the LL.D.

Dr. McConnell started his career as a pastor, where his success, plus the cogency of his writings, focused favorable attention upon him. He was soon called to the presidency of DePauw University. The character of his educational administration gave evidence that if he had remained in that field, he would inevitably have become one of the great educators of America. But in 1912, the General Conference of the Methodist Church elected him to the episcopacy.

As a Bishop, his fame increased. He was pronounced the most incisive intellect in the American pulpit. He was in great demand as a preacher at universities, and has to his credit a number of visiting professorships and lectureships. His qualities of leadership are attested by the fact that he has been President of the Religious Educational Association; President of the Federal Council of Churches of Christ in America; Lyman Beecher Lecturer at Yale, and Barrows Lecturer in India.

He has been prominently identified with movements of social justice, political righteousness, and economic reform. His breadth of view, his tolerance, and his charitable judgments of others make him universally trusted and respected.

FRANCIS J. McCONNELL

The Four Chaplains

IN the early days of World War II, a troop transport (S.S. *Dorchester*), laden to capacity with soldiers, was struck by a torpedo hurled from a submarine. On board were four chaplains. For their bravery, they were posthumously awarded the Distinguished Service Cross, in the citation of which we find these words: "They made their way on deck and began circulating among the troops, 'encouraging them, praying with them and assisting them into lifeboats and life jackets.' . . . Many of the survivors recall seeing the chaplains on the forward deck distributing life jackets from a box. When the box was empty each chaplain removed his own priceless life jacket and gave it to another man. The ship was sinking by the bow when men in the water and in lifeboats saw the chaplains link arms and raise their voices in prayer. They were still on the deck together, praying, when the stricken ship made her final plunge."

Two of these chaplains were Protestant ministers, one was a Roman Catholic priest, and one was a Jewish rabbi. Reading from left to right, they are: George L. Fox, a Methodist preacher; Clark Vandersall Poling, a Dutch Reformed Church preacher; John P. Washington, a Roman Catholic priest; Alexander Goode; a Jewish rabbi.

Chaplain George L. Fox was a graduate of Boston University. He is in this chapel window vicariously for all the alumni of Boston University, living and dead, who have donned their country's uniform in time of war.

Dr. Daniel A. Poling, father of Chaplain Poling, has written a little poem that begins thus:

> "They kept their rendezvous with death
> So valiantly and soon,
> They pledged their youth and gave their all
> And rested at their noon.

[136]

Osmon C. Baker

O SMON CLEANDER BAKER was born in 1812, at Marlow, New Hampshire. His father, Dr. Isaac Baker, and his mother, Abigail Kidder, were both members of prominent old New England families.

Young Osmon entered Wilbraham Academy at fifteen years of age. While a student there, he joined the Methodist Church and dedicated himself to the Christian ministry. He was the first person to matriculate as a student at Wesleyan University, and became the first head of the Newbury Biblical Institute, — the nucleus institution that evolved into Boston University.

By the spring of 1841, Professor Baker and his associates were conducting an extended course of lectures and theological textbook instruction. A year later, the curriculum offerings were enriched, and the *Newbury Biblical Magazine* was issued.

In 1844, Professor Baker resigned to re-enter the pastorate in the New Hampshire Conference; but when the Biblical Institute was transferred to Concord, New Hampshire, he again became a professor, this time of homiletics and Methodist Discipline. He was a born teacher, making upon his students a deep impression both by his unimpeachable character and also by his pedagogically sound and stimulating instruction.

Professor Baker was elected a Bishop of the Methodist Church at the General Conference held in Boston in 1852. He continued to live in Concord until his death nineteen years later. Thus this scholarly, conscientious, kind and competent leader retained an intimate and inspiring relationship with our School of Theology for the first three decades of its existence.

The church spire pictured behind and to the right of Baker in the window is of the church at Newbury, which was the chapel of the embryonic Boston University while it was located there.

[138]

John Dempster

JOHN DEMPSTER was born in 1794, at a town called Florida, in the State of New York.

When he was eighteen years of age, while peddling tin, he came across a Methodist camp meeting. He stopped to scoff, but remained to pray. He had an experimental conversion as truly as had Paul on the Damascus road or Augustine in the garden. His whole life was transformed.

The first thing he did after his conversion was to map out a program of self-education, studying attentively until he became a proficient scholar in the classics, mathematics, theology, philosophy and Hebrew. He began to preach with his religious awakening, and kept at it constantly. After twenty years of effective preaching in New York, he went to South America, and established missions at Buenos Aires, and in other parts of the Argentine. After a stay of six years there, he returned to New York, where he spent three more years in the pastorate.

Then a conviction that had been growing upon him ever since his conversion burst out into bloom and developed into marvelous fruit. It was a conviction that schools should be established for the formal theological education of ministers. His first effort was in connection with the nucleus of Boston University School of Theology. When this institution was moved from Newbury to Concord, it was existing "on a shoestring." John Dempster took hold of the situation with energy and resourcefulness. He collected money for it here and there and everywhere, even visiting England and soliciting funds there. He put the School on a sound economic basis.

In 1854, he became a principal founder of Garrett Biblical Institute, at Evanston, Illinois, and at the time of his death in 1863 he was on the Pacific coast, whither he had gone to establish another theological school.

James E. Latimer

J AMES ELIJAH LATIMER was born at Hartford, Connecticut, the 7th of October, 1826. He was evidently a precocious youngster, being both intelligent and erudite at an unbelievably early age. Although he was ready to enter college when only twelve years old, yet he worked in a dry-goods store until he was eighteen. In his early teens, he experienced a religious awakening. His father, who had at first been a school teacher, had now become a Methodist minister. Young James joined that Church, and dedicated himself to its ministry.

In addition to the formalities of college education, he read more books than any other man known to his companions. He was unexcelled as a mathematician and as a linguist. He studied in Europe. Returning to America, he served a number of the leading pastorates in his Conference. It was natural that he should get into educational work. Every move he made in the educational field was in the nature of a promotion. His final move (in 1870) was into the Professorship of Systematic Theology and the Deanship of Boston University School of Theology, which position he brilliantly filled until his death in 1884.

Bishop William F. McDowell told me once that he regarded it as lamentable that Boston University had failed to make a tradition of Latimer, whom McDowell esteemed as one of the greatest scholars of his day, in any Denomination.

Dean Latimer had a kindly face. He was meticulous in his dress, in his work, in his language, and in his saintliness. He was an eloquent preacher, with something of classical stateliness in his literary style. Being a member of the University Council, he helped President Warren to organize and develop Boston University in its formative period.

[142]

JAMES E. LATIMER

Albert C. Knudson

A LBERT CORNELIUS KNUDSON was born in Minnesota, on the 23rd of January, 1873. I am glad to report that at this writing he is still living.

He took his S.T.B. and Ph.D. degrees from Boston University, meantime studying also in Germany.

Dr. Knudson started his notable teaching career as Professor in the University of Denver; then he moved to Baker University, then to Allegheny College. In 1906, he was called to Boston University School of Theology to teach, first Hebrew and Old Testament Exegesis, and later Systematic Theology.

As a matter of human interest, let me record here that I was elected to the Presidency of Boston University on the 30th of December, 1925, and entered upon the duties of the office on the 1st of February, 1926. In the month that intervened between my election and my assumption of the duties of the office, James A. Beebe, the then Dean of the School of Theology, was elected President of Allegheny College. Hence my first official responsibility on coming into the Presidency of Boston University was to nominate a dean for the School of Theology. I resolved to name the world's most outstanding authority in the field of theological scholarship, and in fulfillment of that resolve, I named Albert C. Knudson.

Dr. Knudson served as the popular and efficient Dean for twelve years, and is at the present time Dean Emeritus. He has written many learned works. His teaching has always been characterized by such thorough scholarship as to win the respect of his students, by such lucidity of expression as to win their admiration, and by such enthusiastic exposition as to make his students evangelists for his subject.

He is a kindly, gracious, and thoughtful gentleman, and a sincere and devout man of God.

[144]

William Fairfield Warren

WILLIAM FAIRFIELD WARREN was born on the 13th of March, 1833, and died on the 6th of December, 1929. Within that long life of nearly ninety-seven years was packed magnificent pioneering educational statesmanship.

When he was a little farm boy of Williamsburg, Massachusetts, he went out one day among the boulders and kindled a fire. When asked why he had done it, he explained that he was afraid God might not notice him, and so he built the fire to attract the attention of the Almighty to his prayer.

Warren was a profound scholar, especially in the fields of cosmogony and cosmology. He studied and taught in Europe. He had sufficient experience in the Methodist ministry to develop the shepherding instinct so essential to a university president. He had been pastor of two of the three men who became Founders of Boston University, and thus exercised a tremendous influence in helping them to decide the best use to make of their fortunes. He had clear ideals for the establishment of a university which would combine the best of English and German universities, and in giving reality to those ideals, he made Boston University the first fully organized American University on a truly university level.

Pictured in the window with President Warren are his son, William Marshall Warren, and his grandson, Shields Warren, — both of them graduates of Boston University. The former was Dean of the College of Liberal Arts for thirty-three years, and is now the revered Dean Emeritus. Shields is an internationally famous scientist, and is a trustee of Boston University. To this Warren tradition must be credited much of the strength of character and quality of service of the University.

William E. Huntington

ILLIAM EDWARDS HUNTINGTON, the second President of Boston University, was born in Hillsboro, Illinois, on the 30th of July, 1844, and died on the 6th of December, 1930.

When this farmer lad was seventeen years old, the Civil War broke out. The Huntington family were followers of Abraham Lincoln, and abolitionists to their finger tips. William enlisted in his country's service. He did not like military life, but Lincoln stirred his loyal heart.

When mustered out, young Huntington enrolled in the University of Wisconsin. He decided to enter the Christian ministry of the Methodist Church, and upon graduation from the University of Wisconsin, matriculated at Boston University School of Theology.

When he was thirty-eight years of age, he was appointed Dean of Boston University College of Liberal Arts, which position he held for twenty-two years. He was a good Dean, combining to a remarkable degree appreciation of academic standards with the disciplinary responsibilities inhering in his office. His students bestowed upon him the sobriquet of the "Dear Dean." Upon the retirement of William Fairfield Warren as President of Boston University, Dr. Huntington was elected to succeed him (11th of January, 1904).

President Huntington was a handsome man, with a good physique. He had a keen sense of humor. Christian gentlemanliness was a dominant characteristic of his life. The indomitable vigor of his religious faith was never abated. He abhorred the low and the profane.

He married into the family of Associate Founder Alden Speare, his first wife being Emma C., and his second wife, Ella M. Speare. They were charming ladies, sisters of our present Treasurer, E. Ray Speare. Dr. Huntington's home life was beautiful.

[148]

Lemuel H. Murlin

L EMUEL HERBERT MURLIN was born in 1861, in the village of
Mendon, Ohio. He died in Greencastle, Indiana, in 1935.

When young Herbert as a boy and youth was not in the country
schools, he was "riding the circuit" with his Methodist preacher
father, jogging along through the deep black muck of the rural roads
of Ohio. The economic condition of the family made it necessary
for each child to become self-supporting at the earliest possible
moment. Lemuel Herbert began clerking in a drug store before he
had finished high school.

After graduating from DePauw, he taught for awhile in the
Preparatory School of DePauw and at the same time served as pastor
of a church. During his pastorate of Knightsville, a new brick church
was erected and named "Murlin Chapel."

When he was thirty-three years of age, and full of hope and
ambition, he was elected President of Baker University. After
seventeen years there, he was elected President of Boston University
to succeed William E. Huntington. Dr. Murlin was a short, stockily
built man, with an open countenance and engaging smile.

He conceived of the University as a municipal institution, — a
delimiting conception that was never held by either of his predeces-
sors nor by his successor. The expansion of Boston University,
under his leadership, reflected the ambitious restlessness of the
country following the First World War. Toward the end of his
administration the acquiring of ground for a new campus was begun;
but because of failing health, President Murlin had neither the
disposition nor the strength to complete the purchase, much less
to undertake the development of the campus. Finally, on the 1st
of January, 1925, the good and faithful servant resigned from the
burdensome Presidency, — and resigned himself to Milton's philosophy that "they also serve who only stand and wait."

[150]

Daniel L. Marsh

THIS medallion is a stained glass reproduction of a photograph taken at the laying of the corner stone of this Chapel. I personally determined the compositions of the other medallions; but this one, I accepted on the recommendation of the architect. He thought that if the globe was an appropriate focal point in Warren's picture, and the book in Huntington's; and if Murlin was environed by the municipality, then the laying of a corner stone might be a suitable motif in the medallion dedicated to the fourth President of the University.

Naturally, only a few persons could be included with the President in so small a space; but those who are here are representative of the multitudinous friends who have made possible the success of the present administration of the University. Reading from left to right, they are: Dr. E. Ray Speare, Treasurer, representing my fellow Trustees and colleagues in the business administration of the University; Dr. Walter G. Muelder, Dean of the School of Theology, representing my colleagues in the faculties and the academic administration of the University; Chester N. Godfrey, executive of the firm of architects whose professional skill has been expertly expressed in the magnificent buildings of which this Chapel is a part. Mr. Godfrey represents not only the architects (Cram & Ferguson) and the builders (Turner Construction Company) but also the non-university part of the community in general. To the right of the central figure is Mrs. Marsh, the elect lady to whom this book is dedicated. I have chosen to have her there not only for her dear self, but also to represent the distaff side of the University family.

If the reader is interested in the history made by the present administration, he is referred to Annual Reports and other records of the University's program and progress for the past quarter of a century.

[152]

The Lectern

THE word "lectern" is derived from the Latin *lectrinum,* which in turn comes from *legere, lectum,* which mean "to read." We use the lectern not merely as a stand or desk from which to read the Bible: it is the visible sign of the spiritual significance of the open Bible, — not "open" literally, or merely open to view; but open in the sense that it is free to be used; that it is without restriction as to the participants, that it is to be revealed, to make known, to be accessible.

The Bible which graces the lectern in this Chapel is a gorgeous volume, gilt-edged, and bound in the finest grade of red morocco. It is printed in beautiful type, large and clear. Engraved in golden letters on the front cover are the words:

Chapel Lectern Bible
BOSTON UNIVERSITY

And inscribed on the inside of the front cover, also in gold, are the following words: "Presented to BOSTON UNIVERSITY by the Massachusetts Bible Society, January 31, 1946, on the occasion of the Dinner commemorating the Twentieth Anniversary of Daniel L. Marsh as President of the University. This Bible is given in anticipation of the Greater University soon to be realized, and in appreciation of the primacy of the Scriptures in the cultural life of the University wherein reverence for the Eternal is held to be the beginning of wisdom."

Carved upon the lectern are the faces of three persons who are forever to be remembered as making the open Bible available to mankind. They are Saint Jerome, John Wycliffe, and Lancelot Andrewes. The parts played by these great men respectively will be indicated in the pages immediately following.

THE LECTERN

Saint Jerome

SAINT JEROME (Eusebius Sophronius Hieronymus) was born
about 380 A.D., on the border of Dalmatia. His parents were
Christians. He received his early education at home. Showing unusual ability as a student, he was sent to Rome where he studied
grammar, rhetoric, law, and philosophy. He was naturally endowed
with the instincts of a true scholar. He spent his Sundays in the
Catacombs discovering and deciphering early Christian records. He
wrote a number of tracts, and traveled widely. He acquired a good
knowledge of Greek and Hebrew.

During an illness, he had a dream which resulted in a profound
spiritual change. It seemed to him as though Christ were rebuking

him for caring more for the flowing rhetoric of Cicero than for the message of the Holy Scriptures. Jerome disliked the unscholarly, uncouth literary style of the Scriptures. He resolved that henceforth he would devote his scholarship to a new translation of the Bible.

When he was about forty years of age, he became acquainted with Pope Damasus. A warm friendship sprang up between them. The Pope was evidently a man of true tolerance and of deep understanding. He encouraged Jerome in preparing an authoritative Latin version of the Holy Bible.

Pope Damasus's successor was not friendly to Jerome personally, and even less friendly to the idea of a popular translation of the Bible. Jerome therefore fled to Palestine, where he entered a monastery. In that Palestinian monastery, he did his monumental life work.

He toiled for twelve years on his great work of translating the entire Bible — the Old Testament out of the Hebrew and the New Testament out of the Greek — into the Latin of the common people.

When his translation appeared, it stirred up the proverbial hornet's nest. A furious storm of protest met it. It is hard to believe that the professional ecclesiastical leadership should be opposed to the common people's having in their vernacular the Word of God, but such was the case.

But truth ultimately triumphed. Jerome's version was soon accepted, and finally became the standard Bible of the Roman Catholic Church, under the terminology of "the Vulgate," or authorized version. It has long since been outmoded in scholarly circles by more authoritative translations, but it was without a peer at the time of its completion, — and until the foregleam of the Reformation heralded the coming of a new and brighter day in Biblical scholarship.

Our sculptor, Mr. Cascieri, has portrayed Saint Jerome in the garb of his time, holding the "Vulgate," the stylus in his hand.

John Wycliffe

OHN WYCLIFFE, the "morning star" of the Reformation, was born in Yorkshire, England, about 1320. At fifteen years of age, he entered Oxford University. There he met scholars who inspired him. He had never had a Bible of his own, for a copy of the Bible at that time cost as much as three yoke of Oxen, — the equivalent of wages received for two hundred forty days' labor.

But at Oxford he became familiar with the Bible. During the twenty-five years following his entrance at Oxford, he became a thoroughly educated gentleman. So great was his success as a teacher that by the time he was forty-one years of age, he was Master of Balliol College, Oxford, and meanwhile a village priest.

[158]

Wycliffe was both learned and courageous. In 1366, he opposed the Pope's claim to tribute so effectively that the demand was never repeated. He fought for reform. He assailed the whole body of ecclesiastics and religious orders for their corruptions. Naturally, he was denounced not only by those whom he criticized, but also by friends, and even by Oxford. When he left his classroom, he was heard to say: "Nevertheless, I think the truth will conquer."

His greatest work was still to be done, namely: the translation of the whole Bible into the English language of the common people. Of course, his translation contained many inaccuracies; but it was the first translation of the Bible into English, and exercised an immeasurable influence upon the making of the English language. Everybody wanted it. Farmers exchanged a load of hay for a few chapters. Crowds of people would gather where one person would read to the whole group.

Wycliffe's belief in the open Bible was both sincere and practical. He trained and sent out itinerant preachers to acquaint Englishmen with its message.

Wycliffe also wrote a number of tracts. He wrote cogently, no longer in Latin, but now in the new tongue that was emerging, the English language. He was as much the founder of English prose as Chaucer was of English poetry.

The influence of Wycliffe's translation of the Bible was tremendous, and the influence of his total contribution to progress was immeasurable.

It was inevitable that any man who in that day would assert national and individual liberty, the preaching of the Gospel to the people, the freeing of the Sacrament of the Lord's Supper from superstition, opposition to the mendicant orders, and who would translate the Bible into English, would be opposed by the hierarchy of the Church. He was denounced, hounded, and finally, in 1384, summoned to appear before the Pope. But before the summons could be answered, the scholarly reformer appeared before a Higher Tribunal. He died on the last day of the year, 1384.

Lancelot Andrewes

LANCELOT ANDREWES was born in London, in 1555, and died at Winchester, in 1626. He was a graduate of Cambridge University. He was richly endowed with brilliant intellectual qualities. He added to his native intellectual ability the virtue of hard work. This was a combination that made his eminence in the field of scholarship inevitable.

In quick succession, he became a teacher in Cambridge, Master of Pembroke Hall, Chaplain to the Queen, Dean of Westminster, Bishop of Chichester, Bishop of Ely, and Bishop of Winchester.

Andrewes was distinguished in many fields. He was a favorite counsellor at court, a recognized scholar, and a great preacher. In his preaching he combined scholarly righteousness with eloquence, which made him a prime favorite. His character was above reproach. He lived a semi-ascetic and wholly self-denying life. He took a prominent, positive, and constructive part in working out the principles of the English Reformation. He published ninety-six sermons.

But great as he was in all the fields suggested above, the greatest reason for mentioning him here is the fact that he is the type and flower of the English scholarship that brought into being the so-called King James Translation of the Bible.

In 1604, King James I called a Council of Puritans and High-churchmen to discuss ecclesiastical affairs. It was decided at this Council that a new and modern translation of the Scriptures was imperative. King James approved of the idea, and did much to promote it. He appointed fifty-four scholars to make the translation. The entire body was divided into three groups, and to each group was assigned a certain portion of the Bible to be translated. The translators began their work in 1607, and faithfully and conscientiously applied themselves to their great task. The new translation was given to the world in 1611. In every edition, it is declared that both the Old and New Testaments were "translated out of the original tongues: and with the former translations diligently compared and revised."

There were fifty-four translators. They were all competent scholars. The first one named — the directing genius of the entire group — was Lancelot Andrewes. His face is carved upon our chapel lectern both in recognition of his great contribution and also vicariously for his colleagues.

Conceding to Wycliffe's translation the formative influence it had upon the English language, yet the fact remains that the King James Version has exercised a more determinative influence than any other book ever written. Truthfully did Lord Macauley once declare: "The English Bible, — a book which if everything else in our language should perish, would alone suffice to show the whole extent of its beauty and power." The translation was made in the era of Shakespeare and Milton, and is in the choicest English of any book ever written in our language. But it is more than a literary gem: It is the Word of God!

Jesus and the Evangelists

U PON the reredos, or screen behind the pulpit, carved in wood
are figures of Jesus and the four Evangelists. A few years
ago, in a General Conference, I came upon a reproduction of Howard
Chandler Christy's artistic conception of Jesus. It was so strong, so
manly, and yet so tender and sympathetic that it strongly appealed
to me. Most artists in trying to picture Jesus are so ambitious to
reveal His pity that they make Him effeminate. But Christy represents Him as strong and masculine, and yet with tears brimming in
His clear blue eyes as He "beheld the city, and wept over it." I suggested to our artist that he might find in Christy something of inspiration for the Christ on the reredos.

This is the same artist that sculptured our statue of John Wesley.
He was equally conscientious in this case; for he studied Christy's
painting not only, but also two hundred other artists' conceptions of
Christ.

With Jesus, who is in the center, are the four Evangelists, —
Matthew and Mark to our left of the Saviour, and Luke and John to
the right.

There are also two other representations of Jesus in the Chapel,
one in the large balcony window of Jesus the Good Shepherd, over
the Commonwealth Avenue entrance, and one in the Rose window
above the chancel. In the pages that follow, you will find these three
representations of Jesus, together with my comments upon them, and
that presentation will be followed by reproductions of the carvings
of the four Evangelists, with my comments upon them.

To Matthew, Mark, Luke and John we are indebted for all we
know of the most wonderful Life that ever blessed this earth. How
poor — how pathetically, how tragically poor — mankind would be
if deprived of the grace, the assurance, the comfort made known in
what Mathew Roydon called "The lineaments of Gospell bookes"!

[162]

The central part of the Chancel, showing the tessellated marble floor in
the foreground, the reredos in the background, and the rose window above.

Jesus Christ

ONCE in a moment of crisis in which Jesus had manifested His poise and power, His disciples exclaimed: "What manner of Man is this?" Let us seek an answer to that question in the Gospels.

He was strong. Strength became Him. He was no namby-pamby plaster saint. He was every inch a man, a man of vigor and strength, — so strong that men instinctively followed Him, and believed in Him, and reverenced Him. Those who were evil hated Him. Those who were good loved Him. He was firm in the right, stronger than the man of oak, stronger than the iron Chancellor.

He was a man of sincerity, — as sincere as honey without wax; so sincere that He hated hypocrisy and lying with all the force of will. He was candid, open-hearted and frank. Men knew that His words meant exactly what they said. He was so far from deceit and trickery and duplicity that He was called *the* Truth!

He was a man of level-headed common sense, — His speech was always characterized by a sweet reasonableness, and His conduct by sound sense.

He was a man of poise. He was poised in the presence of petty and pugnacious emotionalism, calm in the face of calamity, serene when others grew hysterical over ghastly cataclysms.

He was a man of tolerance, — of understanding and good will, of broad ideas and deep sympathies.

He was a man of great friendliness. He befriended the rich and the poor, the privileged and the underprivileged, the good and the bad. The idea of the neighborhood of nations roots in his parable of the Good Samaritan, and the idea of the brotherhood of man gains its real meaning from the life He lived and the Golden Rule He announced.

He was a man of optimism — optimism that was born of His trust

[164]

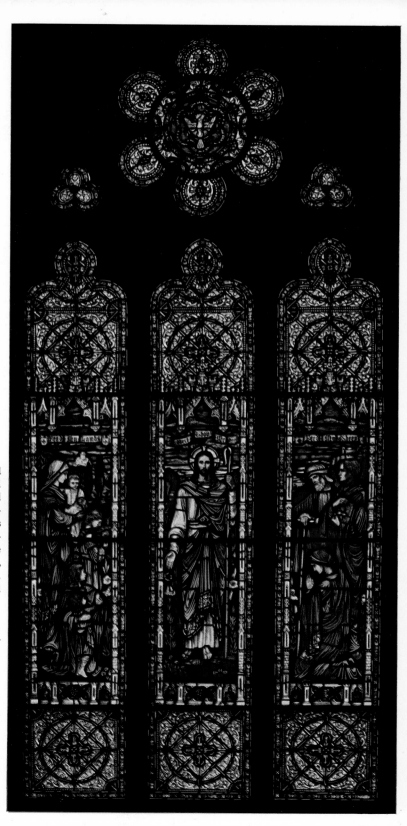

An exquisitely beautiful window: In the central lancet, *"Jesus,* the Good Shepherd," in the left-hand lancet, mothers and children worshiping Jesus, and in the right-hand lancet, adults adoring Him. "Feed my lambs," "Feed my sheep."

in God — optimism that gave Him confidence in others and that gave others confidence in themselves. Recently, a Jewish friend of mine presented me with a complete set of Graetz's monumental six volume *History of the Jews*. Reading it, I was interested to note that this authoritative Jewish historian speaks of Jesus' "intensely sympathetic character," His "high-minded earnestness and spotless moral purity," His "gentle disposition and humility," and declares that Jesus animated poor, helpless and thoughtless people "with His own piety and fervor, and improved their conduct by the hope He gave them of being able to enter the kingdom of heaven."*

He was a man of graciousness, — gracious in His words, courteous in His human contacts, always considerate, kind, gentle.

He was a man of love, — not sickly, simpering sentimentality, but love that desired the welfare of all, and made Him "go about doing good;" love that manifested itself in lavish generosity, in peerless chivalry, in ungrudging forgiveness of offenses and injuries, and even in the sacrifice of Himself for the sake of others. In fact, love is as powerful in the social order He would establish as the atomic bomb is in physical warfare.

He was a man of humility, free from vanity and self-seeking ambition; He was willing to learn from others and from experience; above everything else, He made service to others the standard of true greatness.

He was a man of patience. In contradistinction to the whining, touchy, hair-trigger, or swashbuckler temper, He knew how to bear tribulation uncomplainingly, and how to wait imperturbably for the fulfillment of a plan or purpose.

He was a man of courage, — physical courage, even in Gethsemane and on the cross; intellectual courage, even when He knew that enemies were trying to trap Him; moral courage that kept Him firm for the right, even when weariness and monotony, depression and disillusionment would have made it easy to quit.

He was a man of reverence. His reverence was like a pure white sunbeam which, upon the rain-drops of His deeds and words, shines like a beautiful rainbow, the seven colors of which are respect, defer-

*Graetz: *History of the Jews*, Vol. II, pp. 153, 154.

JESUS

Here our artist, Arcan-
gelo Cascieri, has done
his greatest work. His
face of Christ is strong,
and yet infinitely tender
and kind. The flame
which Christ is holding
is the symbol of His
spirit.

ence, honor, homage, devotion, obedience and veneration. He could not trifle with anything that was sacred.

He believed in the sacred worth of human personality. He believed that every man, woman, and child was valuable, not because of their race or creed, not because of their economic status or social position, but because they were immortal children of God. Therefore, He hated every sin that marred or defaced the image of God in the soul of man. He was opposed to everything that dwarfed or blighted or blasted human personality.

Three names have been given to Jesus that ring in the hearts of men like bells on Christmas day.

The first is "Immanuel," which means "God with us."

The second is: "His name shall be called Wonderful, Counsellor, the Mighty God, the Everlasting Father, the Prince of Peace."

The third: "Thou shalt call His name Jesus: for He shall save His people from their sins." Jesus means Saviour. When Mary was told to call her new born Son by this name, it was a happy augury; for it is the New Testament form of the Old Testament "Joshua," the name borne by the mighty warrior who led Israel into possession of the Promised Land.

Jesus saves from sin by revealing it, condemning it, emphasizing God's eternal hatred of it, making it hideous and loathsome in His all-revealing light. He brings deliverance from it — from its guilt, its defilement, its power. In saving us from sin, He saves us from ignorance and from misery. He cures the sickness of human nature, and heals the breach between God and man.

Well might students pray to Him:

> "Here I train for life's swift race;
> Let me do it in Thy grace:
> Here I arm me for life's fight;
> Let me do it in Thy might."

THE ROSE WINDOW

The North Rose Window pictures the great figure of Christ the Teacher in the medieval tradition of seated posture, clothed in pure white robes, teaching, as it were, the way of Christian life to the people. At His left hand is a symbol of the globe surmounted by the cross, suggesting His domination over the world. In the surrounding petals of the rose are shown symbols of the Eight Beatitudes which Our Lord gave as examples of Christian living, and which He exemplified in His own life. In surrounding tracery shapes are the eight-pointed stars of the Beatitudes. The field is enriched with the grapevine pattern suggesting the unity of the church and the text: "I am the Vine, Ye are the Branches."

All the windows in the Chapel were designed and executed by Charles J. Connick and the Connick Associates of Boston.

Saint Matthew

MATTHEW was doing the despised and unpatriotic job of collecting taxes for the hated Roman government. Jesus passed by where he was sitting at the toll gate, and said: "Follow Me." Matthew arose and followed him.

Matthew was a modest man, and of a retiring nature. It is from the other evangelists that we learn of his farewell feast and about the sacrifice of his property. He was loyal, observant, and faithful. He was familiar with the art of writing from the necessities of his work as a publican. Comparatively speaking, he was a scholar. He had to be acquainted with both the Greek and the Aramaic. In no character do we have more striking evidence of the transforming power of fellowship with Jesus than in the case of Matthew. Before he followed Jesus, he was wholly lacking in patriotism. No one could give more solid evidence of the contempt in which he held Jewish patriotism than by collecting taxes for Rome. After he followed Jesus, he became not only a sincere and devoted disciple and apostle, but he became an exceedingly loyal patriot.

He wrote the Gospel that bears his name for the Jewish people. His Gospel was what Saint Paul afterwards expressed, "the power of God unto salvation, to the Jew first, and also to the Greek." His Gospel begins with a genealogy like the Hebrew histories. It traces the ancestry of Christ to Abraham. It stresses the resemblance of the twelve Apostles to the twelve tribes of Israel.

It is also the Gospel of publicans and tax-gatherers. He has sympathy for all outcasts.

He more than any other records Christ's teaching concerning the Kingdom of Heaven or the Kingdom of God. He gives us the Sermon on the Mount, the Beatitudes, a number of parables consecutively, and a number of miracles consecutively. Keim calls the Gospel according to Saint Matthew the "grand old granite book."

SAINT MATTHEW
Symbol: Angel on Book

Saint Mark

SAINT MARK was socially prominent in the church at Jerusalem. His mother was Mary, a wealthy member of the same church. Peter repaired to her house when released from prison, and found a large crowd of Christians assembled there for worship. Mark was associated with notable men in the history of the early church, particularly with Peter, Paul and Barnabas. He traveled with Peter, and became his interpreter.

Although he may have been personally acquainted with Jesus, yet it was as Saint Peter's interpreter that he acquired the authoritative knowledge which he later put down in the Gospel that bears his name. It is doubtful whether Peter had much knowledge of Greek or of Latin. Mark knew both languages. Therefore when Peter was preaching to the Gentiles, Saint Mark was his interpreter. Peter undoubtedly told the same stories over and over again, until Mark knew them by heart.

Therefore, the Gospel that bears Mark's name is really to be credited as much to Peter as to Mark. The impetuosity of Peter is in it. He wrote largely for the Roman Christians, and his style has in it something of the forcefulness and authoritativeness of the Roman. Matthew is full of discussion, but Mark is full of action. Note how often occur such words as "straightway," "immediately," "forthwith," "shortly," and so on. He gives vivid descriptions of the things with which Peter was personally acquainted, such as the storm at sea, the feeding of the multitude, and the blessing of the children. Thus we have details which point to the testimony of a high witness. The Gospel begins abruptly, without introduction: "The beginning of the gospel of Jesus Christ." It is a hurried narrative all the way, the eager expression of a man who wanted everybody else to get the good news as soon as possible.

SAINT MARK
Symbol: Winged Lion on Book

Saint Luke

LUKE was as congenial to Paul as Mark was to Peter. He was the son of a Greek freedman of a Roman master. He had a good education, both literary and medical. He appears to be a man of modest, tender, sympathetic and loyal nature.

His is the longest of the Gospels, and the most beautiful. Indeed, it has been called the most beautiful book in the world. Luke had a rich vocabulary, and a knowledge of human nature. From the first, his book was "good tidings to all people." It was "a light to lighten the Gentiles." It is a Gospel of far-reaching sympathy for the poor and underprivileged, and this accounts for the emphasis put upon the fact that Mary was a poor peasant girl, the announcement of the Divine Birth to the humble shepherds, the reporting that Jesus took for the text for His first sermon the words of Isaiah: "The spirit of the Lord is upon me, because He hath annointed me to preach good tidings to the poor."

There is sympathy also for the publican, the harlot, the outcast, the penitent thief, the good Samaritan, and the lepers. The very young, and womankind, and the common man all troop into his pages, and upon them all rests the divine nimbus of Christ's sympathy and love.

It is Luke who tells with literary finish the moving parables of the lost sheep, and the lost boy, and the coin lost from a marriage necklace. Reading him, we can feel the solicitude of the shepherd who goes out to find the one sheep that is lost; we can feel the heart-broken anguish of the old father who waits for the prodigal son's return, and we can feel the almost frantic search of the woman for the coin that she had lost from her necklace. Thank God for Dr. Luke who traveled with Paul, and wrote the Book of Acts, and who gleaned every scrap of knowledge concerning Jesus as only a skillful reporter could glean it.

[174]

SAINT LUKE
Symbol: Winged Bull on Book

Saint John

JOHN, the Evangelist: how poor the Christian world would be without his writings! His Gospel glows with the understanding love of the Saviour. It deals chiefly with the spiritual ministry of Christ, and with the inner life of things. It reveals the character of an ambitious, intellectual and courageous man, who, under the influence of Christ, while still strong and courageous became gentle and contemplative. He loved his Lord with passionate devotion.

A dramatic episode in the Saviour's last week summarized the change that had been going on in John's life ever since he became a follower of Jesus, — a change from fire to love, and from ambition to brotherhood. That episode was the washing of the Disciples' feet preceding the Last Supper in the upper room. Jesus heard the jealous jangle and selfish discord of His Disciples as to who should be first in the Kingdom of God. In answer, Jesus performed the most menial service that one person could perform for another, and then announced His great principle that whosoever would be great should serve, and the greatest of all is the servant of all.

The great words of the Gospel according to John are Life, Truth, Witness, Light, Judgment, Believe, Love, Glory.

His Gospel gives us an answer to the question: "What manner of Man is this?" and "What think ye of Christ?" He makes it plain that he knew Jesus personally. The writings of John — the Gospel, the Epistles and the apocalypse — all emphasize the Saviourhood of Jesus, the Fatherhood of God, the brotherhood of man, and self-sacrificing love as the great motive of life. "Beloved, let us love one another." "Little children, love one another." "We love Him, because He first loved us."

The Gospel according to Saint John, from its philosophical beginning to the beautiful climax with which it ends, is a winsome and wistful gospel in the true meaning of the word. It is Good News!

[176]

SAINT JOHN
Symbol: Eagle on Book

Three Great Missionaries

THE large balcony window over the Commonwealth Avenue entrance is an exquisite piece of stained glass art work. The central and dominating figure is that of Jesus the Good Shepherd. The auxiliary lancets on either side illustrate His words: "Feed my lambs" and "Feed my sheep," — on the left, a mother has brought her children to Jesus, and on the right, adults are adoring and worshiping Him.

The bottom part of this window contains pictures of three of the greatest missionaries of all time — Saint Paul, John Eliot, and James W. Bashford.

The first thing a Christian should know is the program of his Lord; for whatever else a person may or may not do, he certainly is not entitled to the sacred name of Christian until he makes his own the program of Jesus, both in bulk and in detail. And yet what an appalling ignorance there is as to the message of Jesus to Mankind!

The old Egyptian priest used to pray: "Ignorant am I, ignorant as Actor, ignorant as Ego, born into ignorance. Lift me from the ocean of ignorance, O Lotus Eyed! Destroy all ignorance, O Destroyer!"

"The primeval sin of humanity," says the ancient Caste, "is being without knowledge."

"My people are destroyed for lack of knowledge," says God through his ancient prophet.

Every prophet of the first order has advanced some creative idea into which has crystallized his message to mankind. Jesus Christ has His own message, and it crystallizes into a favorite idea: "the kingdom of God." It is the heart of His message to the world.

What a tremendous dream of world empire Christianity cherishes at its heart! Its marching orders are, "Ye shall be my witnesses unto the uttermost part of the earth." The person who does not believe in Christian missions is hardly entitled to be called a believer in the

Christian religion; for its massive imperial word is "Go . . . to the whole creation."

But Christianity is more than a dream. It is a series of events. It has translated the luminous, gripping message of the Gospel into every language and into the very terms of the experience of every race and of every type of man. It is diffusing a great moral compulsion. It is releasing upon all the world a vast spiritual momentum. It is saturating the human mind with the ideals and principles of Jesus Christ. Its by-products in government, literature, art, and science are beyond computation.

"Unto the uttermost parts of the earth" Christian missions have gone preaching, teaching, and healing. The missionaries are pioneers of conquest. The missionary movement is Christianity in action.

Let students who view the pictures of the great missionaries in our Chapel windows consider seriously the stewardship of life and of substance. Such consideration will tend to bring God out of the region of abstraction and make Him real. An intelligent conviction concerning the stewardship of life will cause the finest and most talented young people of the church to offer themselves for the great serving positions of the church at home and abroad.

Saint Paul

SAINT PAUL, with a swordlike question, laid bare the *raison d'etre* of Christian missions, thus: "For whosoever shall call upon the name of the Lord shall be saved. How then shall they call on him in whom they have not believed? and how shall they believe in him of whom they have not heard? and how shall they hear without a preacher? And how shall they preach, except they be sent? as it is written, how beautiful are the feet of them that preach the gospel of peace, and bring glad tidings of good things!"

His own life furnished the inevitable answer to those questions. He made a total of three missionary tours in which he covered the whole western world so far as it was known in his day. His immortal Epistles were written as a by-product of his missionary work. His life is a glorious example of consecration to a Person and of devotion to an ideal, and of fortitude and enduring patience.

Paul's missionary achievement was an epic, — an Odyssey and Iliad combined. His life was a constant wandering like that of Ulysses. It was a succession of conflicts and victories. He marched breast forward: There was no retreat in his warfare. Paul was the Attorney General of Christianity before the Bar of the World. He was a statesman who laid broad and deep foundations of a Christian empire. Wherever people were to be saved, there Paul went to labor and to preach.

> "The Son of God goes forth to war;
> A kingly crown to gain;
> His blood-red banner streams afar:
> Who follows in His train?
> Who best can drink his cup of woe,
> Triumphant over pain,
> Who patient bears his cross below,
> He follows in His train."

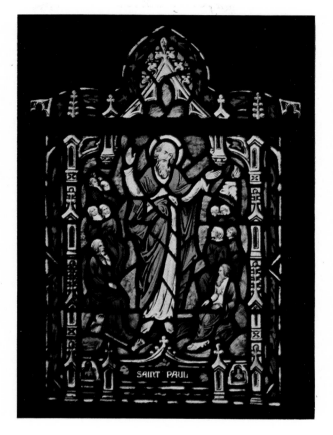

SAINT PAUL

"I was not disobedient unto the heavenly vision; but
shewed first unto them of Damascus, and at Jerusalem,
and throughout all the coasts of Judea, and then to the
Gentiles, that they should repent and turn to God, and
do works meet for repentance."

John Eliot

JOHN ELIOT, the famous "Apostle to the Indians" was born in England in 1604, and died in Massachusetts eighty-six years later. After being educated at Cambridge University, he started out as a clergyman in the Established Church of England; but before long he became an usher at the School of Rev. Thomas Hooker. Under the influence of Hooker, he became a Puritan, and emigrated to America when twenty-seven years of age.

The illiterate and pagan condition of American Indians kindled in Eliot's soul an unquenchable fire of missionary zeal. He mastered the dialect of the Indians in the neighborhood of Boston so that he might translate the Bible into their vernacular and teach them to read. First he translated the Ten Commandments and the Lord's Prayer, and preached to the Indians in their own tongue. Many of the Indians were converted to the Christian faith, which resulted in the incorporation of the "Society for the Propagation of the Gospel in New England." Eliot continued his work until he had translated the entire Bible, and established Christian Indian colonies in what are now Roxbury, Newton, Natick, and Stoughton, and inspired missionary work on behalf of the Indians also on the islands of Martha's Vineyard and Nantucket.

King Philip's War dealt a staggering blow to Eliot's work; but Eliot's vision, devotion and consecration will stand forever in beautiful contrast to much that was sordid in the relationship of the white Europeans and the American red Indians.

Eliot intelligently and consecratedly gave to the untutored Indian the light which illuminated his own soul.

> "Can men, whose souls are lighted
> With wisdom from on high,
> Can they to men benighted
> The lamp of life deny?

JOHN ELIOT

In a letter to Charles II, accompanying a copy of the
Bible which he presented to the monarch, Eliot states:
"We present this, and other concomitant fruits of our
poor endeavors to plant and propagate the gospel here,
which upon a true account is as much better than Gold
as the Souls of men are worth than the whole world."

James W. Bashford

JAMES Whitford Bashford was born in Wisconsin in 1849, and
died in California in 1919. Like Paul, he was an intellectual, a
statesman, a theologian; like Eliot, he was an indefatigable worker,
a believer in the educability of all, and an educator in the truest
sense of the word.

Bashford took his Bachelor of Sacred Theology and his Doctor of
Philosophy degrees at Boston University. After experience in the
pastorate, he was made President of Ohio Wesleyan University.
His success there led inevitably to his election as a Bishop of the
Methodist Church, in 1904, for missionary work in China.

In his work in China, he displayed a vast endowment of common
sense, intelligence, tact, consecrated zeal, and far-seeing statesmanship. Under Bashford's inspiring leadership, most of the creators of
the then new Republic of China became Christians and members of
the Methodist Church. He was their confidential adviser. He also
urged upon President Taft in 1912 the recognition of the Chinese
Republic. He secured a copy of Japan's secret Twenty-one Demands
in 1915; and after careful study of the demands, communicated to
the United States Government the gravity of the situation. That
same spring, President Wilson and Secretary of State Bryan called
Bashford into closeted conference with them.

The last time I saw Bishop Bashford, he was coughing excruciat-
ingly, but with indomitable will he swayed a meeting in favor of an
aggressive missionary policy for the Far East. He made me think
of words uttered by his beloved China's Confucius in a moment of
self-revelation: "This is the character of the man, so intent upon en-
lightening the eager that he forgets his hunger, and does not realize
that old age is at hand."

> " 'Are ye able,' said the Master,
> 'To be crucified with me?—'
> 'Yea,' the sturdy dreamers answered,
> 'To the death we follow Thee.' "

[184]

JAMES W. BASHFORD

"The divine purpose contemplates the evangelization of all peoples in pagan lands and the complete Christianization of the races. . . . I have dared to sow, the harvest will test the seed, and also the soil. Let us pray God that the seed prove sound, the soil good, and the harvest a hundredfold."

The Organ

THE organ, made by Casavant Brothers Limited, in Quebec, Canada, is adjudged by competent critics to be one of the finest organs in this part of the country. It is the gift to Boston University of the Honorable Guy W. Cox.

Mr. Cox is a delightful combination of erudition and business acumen. He is a graduate of Dartmouth College and of Boston University School of Law. After a distinguished career as a lawyer and a public servant, he became first the legal Counsel and then the President of the John Hancock Mutual Life Insurance Company. This company is one of the strongest financial institutions in the world. It has over ten billions of dollars of insurance in force.

Hand carved organ screens on both sides of the chancel add to its chaste beauty.

For a number of years Mr. Cox directed its affairs with social efficiency, business shrewdness, and administrative skill.

At the same time, Mr. Cox is instinctively a scholar. He reads for sheer intellectual enjoyment the profoundest works on philosophy and kindred subjects. For mental recreation, he reads in the original Latin the poems of Horace, Ovid, Vergil and other Roman authors.

Mr. Cox has been a trustee of Boston University for many years, and has also been Chairman of its Board of Trustees. The first time I ever saw Mr. Cox was when he was playing a cottage organ at the wedding of the daughter of the late United States Senator William Butler, at Senator Butler's summer home on Martha's Vineyard Island. He was performing this service not only because he and Senator Butler were dear friends, but also because he is an organist of no mean ability.

The name of this public-spirited and cultured gentleman will be held in grateful remembrance by successive generations of Boston University personnel because of his gift of this organ.

There are several carved panels on the organ screens, including representations in the central panels, of Saint Gregory, with dove on shoulder, holding a monochord, and Saint Cecelia holding a portable organ. On the other panels are figures of bells, lyre, clef scrolls and music staffs.

Saint Gregory rates recognition on this Chapel organ because of the traditional work he did on the liturgy of the Church, and particularly because, when he was Pope, he not only sent missionaries to the British Isles but also sent with them a large number of selected and arranged melodies. These songs, or chants, were taught by the missionaries to the natives, and became uniform throughout the kingdom. To this day the Gregorian chant perpetuates his name in musical circles.

Saint Cecelia is the patron saint of music. She is credited with having praised God by instrumental and vocal music. Traditions concerning her have been the inspiration of many masterpieces in art, including works by Raphael, Domenichino, Dolce and Mignard. In the Roman Catholic Church, her festival (22nd of November) is celebrated with beautiful music.

[188]

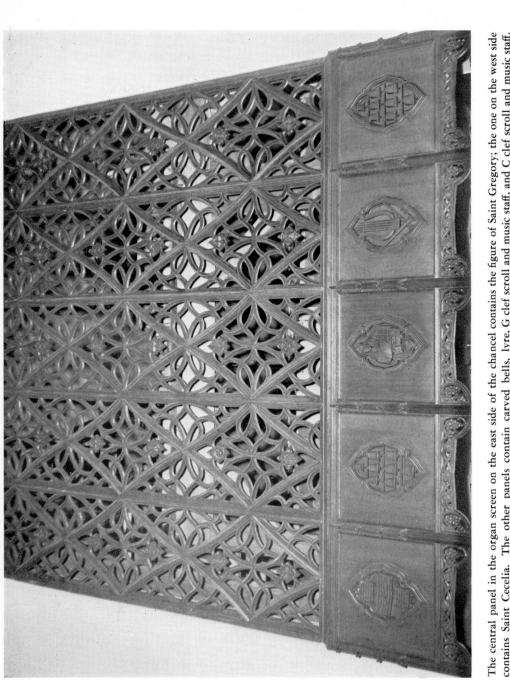

The central panel in the organ screen on the east side of the chancel contains the figure of Saint Gregory; the one on the west side contains Saint Cecelia. The other panels contain carved bells, lyre, G clef scroll and music staff, and C clef scroll and music staff.

Saint Cecelia is by some regarded as the inventor of the organ. This is erroneous; for the organ was developed, several centuries before she was born, from the most primitive form of Pan-pipes, —tufts of reeds that grew along the water's edge. Nevertheless, Cecelia's story forms one of Chaucer's *Canterbury Tales,* and her fame makes her the symbol of sweet music, both vocal and instrumental.

Let this Chapel become famous for its music. Let patriotic "music swell the breeze." Let songs of comfort soothe the sorrowing. Let the wedding march set the hearts of lovers in rhythmic beat with truth and trust to go through life together without a rift in the lute of their love. Let students sing:

> "Almighty Lord, with one accord
>   We offer Thee our youth,
> And pray that Thou would'st give us now
>   The warfare of the truth."

Above all, let us sing most of and to Him whom Saint Cecelia and Saint Gregory honored:

> "O could I speak the matchless worth,
> O could I sound the glories forth
>   Which in my Saviour shine,
> I'd sing His glorious righteousness,
> And magnify the wondrous grace
>   Which made salvation mine.
>
> "I'd sing the characters He bears,
> And all the forms of love He wears,
>   Exalted on His throne:
> In loftiest songs of sweetest praise,
> I would to everlasting days
>   Make all His glories known."

The Bells

THE carillonic bells — twenty-five English bells and sixty-one Flemish bells — have been installed to ring their glad music not only within the Chapel but over the campus as well. These bells were the gift of the trustees of Boston University as individuals, not as a corporate body.

The names of all the effective trustees and all the honorary trustees have been inscribed upon a bronze plaque not only to perpetuate their names to posterity, but also to testify to future members of the University family that the spirit of unanimity and coöperation which has characterized the trustees during the past quarter of a century has been as sweet and harmonious as any music made by these bells can ever be.

As the bells sound forth over the campus and across the historic Charles River, let them be heard as Longfellow

> ". . . heard the bells on Christmas Day
> Their old, familiar carols play,
>   And wild and sweet
>   The words repeat
> Of peace on earth, good-will to men!"

Let them ring out as Tennyson exhorted the bells of his day:

> "Ring out old shapes of foul disease,
>   Ring out the narrowing lust of gold;
>   Ring out the thousand wars of old,
> Ring in the thousand years of peace!

> "Ring in the valiant man and free,
>   The larger heart, the kindlier hand!
>   Ring out the darkness of the land,
> Ring in the Christ that is to be!"

Bach

"ALL deep things are Song," says Carlyle in his *Heroes and Hero Worship.* "It seems somehow the very central essence of us, Song; as if all the rest were but wrappages and hulls! The primal element of us; of us, and of all things."

Jennie Lind, the sweet singer whose chosen symbol was the lark — the lark that "singing ever soars," and "soaring ever sings" — urged us not to make an idol of music but to "place it at the foot of the Cross, laying all our longings, sufferings, joys and expectations in a light of a dying and risen Saviour!"

How appropriate, then, that on the posts of the chancel railing which mark the entrance to our chapel choir should be carved the features of two of the greatest composers of church music in the world, Bach and Handel.

Johann Sebastian Bach was born in 1685, at Eisenach, Germany. He was left an orphan at ten years of age. The next five years of his life were under the guidance of his elder brother. That elder brother was interested in music, and Johann Sebastian was nothing short of a genius in music. The elder brother was evidently jealous of his young protégé, and forbade him to continue copying the great musical compositions. The youngster, driven with an insatiable hunger for musical knowledge, continued his copying at nighttime, with no light except the light of the moon which filtered through his latticed window. This so injured his eyes that he had impaired vision for the rest of his life, and went blind in his last year.

When Johann Sebastian was fifteen years old, his brother died. Shortly thereafter, Johann became a church organist, and a choirmaster for the Duke of Weimar. His genius was being recognized, and others were encouraging him and opening doors of opportunity for him.

He removed to Leipzig, where he was a church organist — the greatest organist of his era. He also composed, while at Leipzig, his great church music, a number of choral pieces, and above everything else, his colossal achievement: "The Passion According to Saint Matthew." There was something expansive, subtle, and universal in his musical compositions. His art expressed everything that was good. While he wrote in various fields, it was in the field of church music that he excelled. He composed one hundred ninety church cantatas, four short masses, and three wedding cantatas — Easter Oratorio, Christmas Oratorio, and the "Passions According to Saint Matthew and Saint John."

Bach died of apoplexy when he was sixty-five years of age. He was a hard worker. He was goaded to achievement by an almost childlike faith, using his art to interpret the infinite. He summed up his own attitude by declaring that "the objective of all music should be to glorify God." And Schumann summed Bach up in these words: "Music owes as much to Bach as a religion to its founder."

Handel

GEORG FRIEDRICH HANDEL was born in 1685, at Halle, Germany. Modern music began with Bach and Handel. By coincidence, they were born the same year. Their birthplaces are not far apart.

Handel's father was a barber-surgeon. Georg Friedrich was a precocious musician. His father opposed music as a career; but the youngster smuggled into his attic a clavichord (a musical instrument that cannot be heard when played behind closed doors), and practiced upon it. In time, the father was prevailed upon to withdraw his objections to Georg's study of music, and the youngster then began in earnest under a competent teacher.

[194]

In his teens, he went to Hamburg and became acquainted with Matheson, a composer and writer of music. They were mutually helpful friends; but once they had a quarrel which culminated in a duel, and Handel would have been killed had it not been that Matheson's sword struck a large button on Handel's coat, which prevented its piercing his heart.

His first opera, "Almira," was performed when he was twenty years of age. He spent three years in Italy, a couple of years in England, another year or so in Germany, then went to England where he became a naturalized Englishman. He was bluff and hearty in character. Both he and Bach had the characteristic virtues of the German Lutheran — hard work, unscrupulous honesty, seriousness of purpose.

Handel wrote many operas and oratorios, mostly on Biblical themes, such as Esther, Deborah, Belshazzar, Judas Maccabaeus, Joshua, Solomon, and the great choral work, "Israel in Egypt."

It is said that when his "Messiah" was first performed in London, the King was present, and was so deeply stirred by it that when the "Hallelujah Chorus" was being sung, the King arose and stood reverently at attention, whereupon all the rest of the audience arose. From then until now, it has been the custom for the audience to rise at the singing of the "Hallelujah Chorus." The respectful treatment accorded it would seem to make the "Hallelujah Chorus" the national anthem of the Kingdom of God on earth.

Appropriately does the Boston University Chorus sing at each Christmas Convocation the "Hallelujah Chorus" from "The Messiah":

> "Hallelujah!
> For the Lord God omnipotent reigneth.
> The kingdom of this world is become
> The kingdom of our Lord, and of His Christ;
> And He shall reign for ever and ever,
> King of Kings, and Lord of Lords!
> Hallelujah!"

The Marbles Come from Afar

THERE are many things about the Chapel which make it a protest against provincialism. If you desire proof, ascertain how many different countries are represented in the materials from which are made the broadcasting and amplifying apparatus. Find out where the various materials and parts of the carillonic bells originated. Remember that the organ was made in Canada. Look at the lovely chandeliers that light the Chapel, and seek out the sources of the various materials composing them.

A list of marbles used in the Chapel is interesting. The floor of the Nave and Narthex is unfading dark mottled green and purple marble from Vermont. There are four different kinds of marbles in the communion rail step — alternating diamonds of Italian red Levanto and Vermont verde antique in a field of pink Tennessee with a border of Belgian black marbles.

The main chancel floor has a center diamond of Rojo Alicante marble from Spain, surrounded by two borders, the inner one being pink Tennessee, and the outer one red Levanto. These are set in a field of alternating diamonds of Vermont verde antique and pink Tennessee with a border of Belgian black. The rest of the chancel floor has fields of pink Tennessee and Belgian black borders. All the chancel risers are of pink Tennessee with Belgian black treads.

The marbles relate us to a long geologic past and have durable qualities for a long future; but as Daniel Webster says:

> "If we work upon marble, it will perish. If we work upon brass, time will efface it. If we rear temples, they will crumble to dust. But if we work upon men's immortal minds, if we imbue them with high principles, with the just fear of God and love of their fellow men, we engrave on those tablets something which no time can efface, and which will brighten and brighten to all eternity."

[196]

Meditation Chapel

O N the ground floor of our Chapel are several smaller rooms, the most important of which is the "Meditation Chapel." It has about one-fifth the capacity of the main chapel, and is intended both for smaller services and also as a place of meditation for students, faculty members, and friends who feel in the mood for quiet thought.

This Meditation Chapel has been established as a memorial to the late Rev. Dr. Millard Lyman Robinson, by his wife, Edna Stitt Robinson. Dr. Robinson was a graduate of Boston University three times over — A.B., S.T.B., Ph.D.

He was a big man by every measurement. He was a good preacher and a good administrator. A large part of his effective ministry was spent as Executive Secretary of the New York City Society of the Methodist Church, and later as General Secretary of the New York Bible Society.

He had a character as solid and reliable as the granite in the hills of his native Westfield, Massachusetts. He personalized the good old-fashioned virtues and pieties. He was loyal to his country, his church, his university, and his friends. Millard and I were friends for many years. I loved him and trusted him, and rejoice to have his name associated with this Chapel.

His life of service, truth, and worship is properly commemorated in this Meditation Chapel; for the three windows over the chancel bear the captions of *Service, Truth,* and *Worship.* They will be separately pictured and discussed in the pages immediately following.

Meditation is to our reading what digestion and assimilation are to our food. Meditation means that we resolve the great truths of religion in our mind. It is our right and our duty to examine ourselves. The person who never takes inventory of his spiritual stock in trade is headed straight for bankruptcy.

Service

SERVICE is a hard-worked word. Even the abridged form of Webster's New International Dictionary gives it twenty different definitions. Of course, the sense in which the word is used here is spiritual service as shown by obedience, good works, and love.

Jesus was the great exemplar of service. He was meek and lowly and humble. By His dramatic act of washing His disciples' feet — an act in which he performed the most menial service possible — He showed that humility is not meanness of spirit, self-depreciating speech, nor inverted pride. When He said, "I have given you an example," He made forever luminous the truth that service is the standard of real greatness, and that true humility is a disposition to serve. It is the key to the highest service. It dignifies and glorifies service. Sir Walter Scott says that the most beautiful scenery in Scotland is not in the Highlands nor yet in the Lowlands, but at the meeting of the two. So also, the path of lowly service becomes the highway of God.

Those who knew Jesus best said that "He went about doing good." If we would follow Him, we also must go about doing good continuously, — doing good until oppression, and avarice, and gaunt famine, and poverty are gone; until all children have a chance for God-like development; until the inferno of every city slum has been purified, and every disease-infested tenement has been torn down; until all sickness is cared for, and all hunger fed, and all nakedness clothed; until the worn, pinched, pale faces of the underprivileged and dispossessed are illumined with inner joy, and until stunted growth has been coaxed into flower and fruitage. We are to go about doing good in meekness and lowliness of heart, in the beauty of conduct, in the sublime exactions of morality; by gentle, lucid and courageous speech; by judicious and heroic silence; by patience, and fortitude, and faith; by forbearance and by deed.

[198]

SERVICE

The allegorical figure of Service bears the words of
the Saviour: "Inasmuch as ye have done it unto one
of the least of these my brethren, ye have done it
unto me." Below the allegorical figure is depicted
the Parable of the Good Samaritan
(Saint Luke 10:25-37).

Truth

TRUTH and troth have the same root. John Horne Tooke declares: "Truth is that which a man troweth." Troth means pledged faith or fidelity. Truth is reality, genuineness, sincerity.

Jesus declared, "Ye shall know the truth and the truth shall make you free." Opinions are nothing more than prejudice until they become a part of our own experience and thought. Truth is moral and practical as well as intellectual.

The ancient Egyptians regarded truth as "the main cardinal virtue." Plato taught that "the genuine lie is hated by all gods and men." In Saint John's vision of the city of God, he noted that traitors to the truth were left outside with other despicable characters: "Without are the dogs and the sorcerers and the fornicators and the murderers and the idolaters and everyone that loveth and maketh a lie."

All science rests upon inviolable truth. The very core of the scientific spirit is the search for truth. Chinese Gordon once wrote to his sister: "If you tell the truth, you have infinite power *supporting* you; but if not, you have infinite power *against* you."

Truth cannot be destroyed. If one puts himself on the side of Truth and Right, he may rest assured that he is on the side that will ultimately triumph.

We must not tamper with the truth in any form. We must encourage it in science, letters, art, and religion. No man should be permitted to defile it by interpreting it for selfish ends. And we must enthrone as King of our lives Him who said: "I am the truth." He was the truth concerning man, revealing to us how wretchedly far short we fall of what we ought to be. And He was the truth concerning God, revealing His love that yearns to save us from ourselves and from our sins.

[200]

TRUTH

The allegorical figure of Truth is represented as
holding the open Bible, on which are the words of
Jesus: "Ye shall know the truth, and the truth shall
make you free." The lower part of the window
depicts three persons searching the Scriptures as
recorded in the Acts of the Apostles 17:11. The
reference is to Paul's visit to Thessalonica.

Worship

OUR word "worship" is derived from two Anglo-Saxon words which mean worth-shape. The original users of the word were trying to say that when a man bows before the great I AM, he assumes a worthy shape.

We all need to worship at all times, especially in this day of bewilderment. It is through worship that the soul goes in quest of its counterpart. It is through worship that we are enabled to see the eternal in the temporal, the permanent beyond the transient, and the invisible through the visible. Worship tends to give us a sense of proportion and a sense of values. It helps us to see that which is little as little and that which is big as big. It gives us strength to jingle in the ear of eternity the coin that the world offers us in exchange for our souls. The man who truly worships cultivates serenity in the face of calamity, and poise in the presence of petty and pugnacious emotionalism. The true worshiper builds his house of life philosophy upon a solid rock, and hence it will stand though the storms of ghastly cataclysm and political intrigues beat all about it. The worshiper lifts his eyes to the far horizon and takes the long forward look. He sees life whole, taking in the long course of history to which his single life and this vast world belong. He worships Him who encompasses all centuries and all places in His mind and purpose.

Worship energizes man's will to be what he ought to be and to do what he knows he ought to do. Through worship, a tide of spiritual refreshment comes welling and surging in from the ocean of God's mercy, and helps us to keep alive spiritually in a crassly materialistic age.

WORSHIP

The allegorical figure of Worship bears the great
words of Jesus: "God is a Spirit, and they that worship Him must worship Him in spirit and in truth."
Below is a picture of Jesus in the Garden of Gethsemane. The Scriptural reference is
Saint Luke 22:40-44.

The Name of the Chapel

I HAVE left until the end the name of the Chapel. I am sure the reader will allow me to make a simple and sincere statement concerning it.

Several suggestions for attaching the President's name to the campus were made from the beginning of the campus development. All these suggestions, I vetoed. I did so not out of any excess of modesty, but simply because I sincerely did not desire that it should be done. However, when the contract was let for the Chapel, and its construction had been started, again the proposal was made that the Chapel should be known as the Marsh Chapel. Attention was called to the fact that it stood at the geographical center of the campus; that it occupied ground that had once been a street which had been donated to the University by the city, on the initiative of the President; that it symbolized the unity of the University, to which consummation the President had consecrated himself from the beginning, and that it symbolized the centrality of religion in education, in which the President so profoundly believed.

I still demurred, until it was suggested that I follow certain worthy precedents, including the following: Lowell House at Harvard University was so named while A. Lawrence Lowell was still President of that famous institution. One of the noblest bridges spanning the Charles River, connecting the cities of Boston and Cambridge, is called the Larz Anderson Bridge, and it had been named for Mr. Anderson, not only with his consent, but largely on his own initiative. Hoover Dam was named for Herbert Hoover while he was President of the United States, and hence he was charged with the responsibility of either approving or disapproving of the name. He approved! Mount McKinley in Alaska was named for William McKinley while he was President of the United States, — and it was so named with his approval. The most convincing historical precedent had to do with George Washington, one of the greatest men of all time, and a man in whom modesty was a sovereign characteristic. I was reminded that on a blustery day in 1791, George Washington, at that time President of the United States, rode with six other horsemen over the site of the city that was to bear his name. All day long Washington and his companions threshed through thickets and floundered through swamps beside the Potomac River. All day long, Major L'Enfant regaled Washington with the glories that were to be in the city that would rise on this site, bearing the name of Washington, with Washington's unaffected approval.

In the light of such precedents, I concluded that maybe I was smugly mistaking inverted pride for modesty. Let the rest of the story be told by the following excerpt from the official Minutes of the regular meeting of the Trustees of Boston University held on the 14th of March, 1949:

Chairman Cox then announced that Walter G. Muelder, Dean of the School of Theology, and Atlee L. Percy, Dean of the University, were present as a delegation appointed by the University Council, with request for privilege to present a matter to the Trustees. This privilege was granted, and Dean Muelder read the following communication, to-wit:

"To the Trustees of Boston University:

"The Boston University School of Theology Faculty at a recent meeting unanimously adopted a recommendation which the Dean of that School was requested to present to the University Council, with the expressed hope that the Council would add its endorsement to the recommendation, and pass it on to the Trustees of Boston University. The action of the Faculty of the School of Theology is stated in the following letter to President Marsh:

'For over twenty years you have been the spirited leader of the University in an effort to bring on one unified campus

[205]

the many schools and colleges of Boston University. The fulfillment of this great conception is now taking place and can
be appreciated by all. There have been times when you alone
carried the vision through days of doubt and discouragement
among many. You are an alumnus of Boston University
School of Theology and have diligently conserved the values
of theological education so that the School of Theology has
been not only a distinguished part of Boston University, but
has become one of the nation's great theological seminaries.
The faculty of the School of Theology, therefore, wish to
recommend to the University Council, and through them to
the Board of Trustees, that the new Chapel be named The
Marsh Chapel. It is our unanimous and enthusiastic recommendation that you should be thus permanently recognized
in the future development of the new campus.

'We do not wish to impose this recommendation on you
should you for any reason wish to have the chapel named for
some donor, but assuming that no special circumstance should
arise for naming the chapel, the faculty of the School of
Theology covet the honor of recommending that your magnificent devotion to religion and to learning be recognized by
naming the chapel Marsh Chapel.'

"When this suggestion came to the University Council,
the members of the Council unanimously and with enthusiasm endorsed the idea but added to it the conviction that
the chapel not only but also the tower which is to stand at
the center of the campus so close to the chapel as to be to all
intents and purposes a part of it, should also be named
for President Marsh. The University Council appointed
Deans Muelder and Percy to formulate their recommendation and present it to the Trustees of Boston University,
which we hereby gladly do, suggesting the following resolutions for consideration and adoption by the Trustees:

"RESOLVED that the Boston University Chapel which is
to stand at the center of the campus, contract for which
has already been let to the Turner Construction Company,

shall be called The Daniel L. Marsh Chapel, and shall be properly marked as such, said marking to be satisfactory to President Marsh and approved by him.

"IT IS FURTHER RESOLVED that when the administrative tower, which from the beginning has been the dominant architectural motif of the development program, and which is to be built at the northern end of the chapel and is architecturally a part of the chapel, shall have been constructed, it also shall be known as The Daniel L. Marsh Tower, thus making the chapel and its tower a monument to our President's constructive administration of the University's progress.

"At the President's request, it is agreed that in the event a gift should be made in the amount of the cost of the tower, or in any amount totaling more than one-half the cost thereof, then the tower may be named for whatever person or persons the donor may designate, with the approval of the President and Trustees of the University."

The resolutions were greeted by applause and approving comments by the Trustees, and it was then

UNANIMOUSLY VOTED, by a standing vote (President Marsh alone not voting), that the foregoing resolutions be and hereby are adopted.

As you will see, a few words were selected from the foregoing record to form the concise statement which has been inscribed over the main entrance to the Chapel, as follows:

BY ORDER OF THE TRUSTEES OF BOSTON UNIVERSITY, THIS CHAPEL IS NAMED FOR PRESIDENT MARSH IN PERMANENT RECOGNITION OF HIS SPIRITED LEADERSHIP AND OF HIS MAGNIFICENT DEVOTION TO RELIGION AND TO LEARNING.

The Charm of the Chapel

✠

Religious Leaders Commend It

"THE CHARM OF THE CHAPEL is a story charmingly told in classic prose, and reveals another facet of the multiplied talents of the distinguished educator for whom the chapel is named. It will be read with delight by all who love the good, the true, and the beautiful." — G. BROMLEY OXNAM, *Bishop of the Methodist Church*

"THE CHARM OF THE CHAPEL is a beautiful piece of work. The book is beautifully done and will make a valuable contribution towards sweetening the atmosphere of a secularist age." — RICHARD J. CUSHING, *Archbishop of Boston (Roman Catholic)*

"I find THE CHARM OF THE CHAPEL inspiring in many different aspects, . . . coupled with the very wide sense of friendship and toleration for all who share the great basic ideals of Judaism and Christianity. .The beautiful illustrations, especially of the stained glass windows, make the book a true aesthetic delight." — S. BRODETSKY, *President of the Hebrew University, Jerusalem*

"The author's description is not only a thing of artistic delight but also a deft touch revealing his deep faith and character. Who reads this book with its ideals and descriptions will be the wiser and better for it." — J. R. CUNNINGHAM, *President of Davidson College and former Moderator of the General Assembly of the Presbyterian Church in the U. S.*